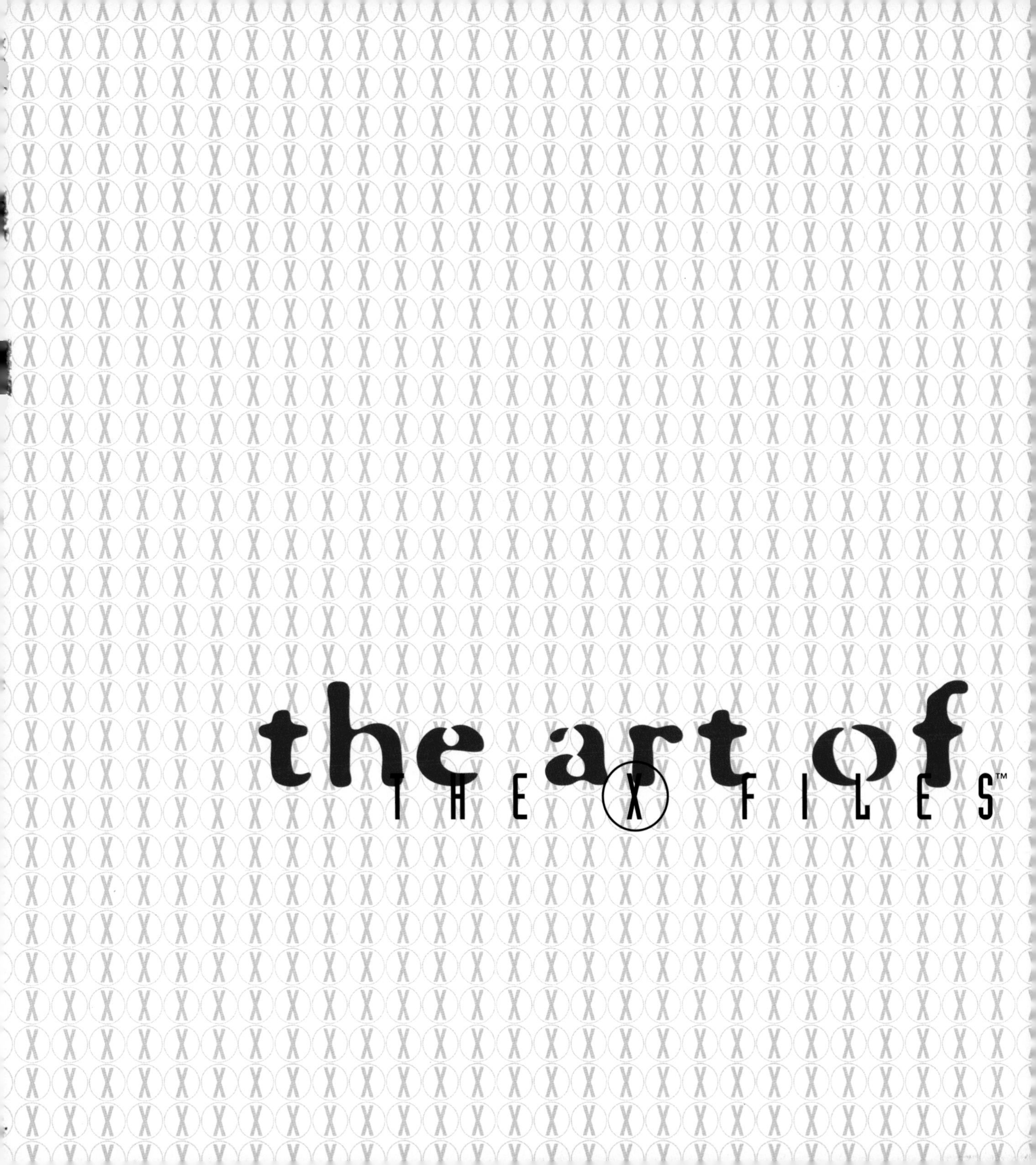
the art of
THE X FILES™

Packagers/Editors: Marvin Heiferman, Carole Kismar

Project Director: Meryl Holland

Designer: Tanya Ross-Hughes/Hotfoot Studio

Art Coordinator: Kathy Brew

Assistant Editors: Will Montoya Caperton,

David Hughes/Hotfoot Studio, Mira Jacob

A Lookout Book / The M. Company & Friends

Voyager

An Imprint of HarperCollins*Publishers*

Inspired by *The X-Files*™, created by Chris Carter

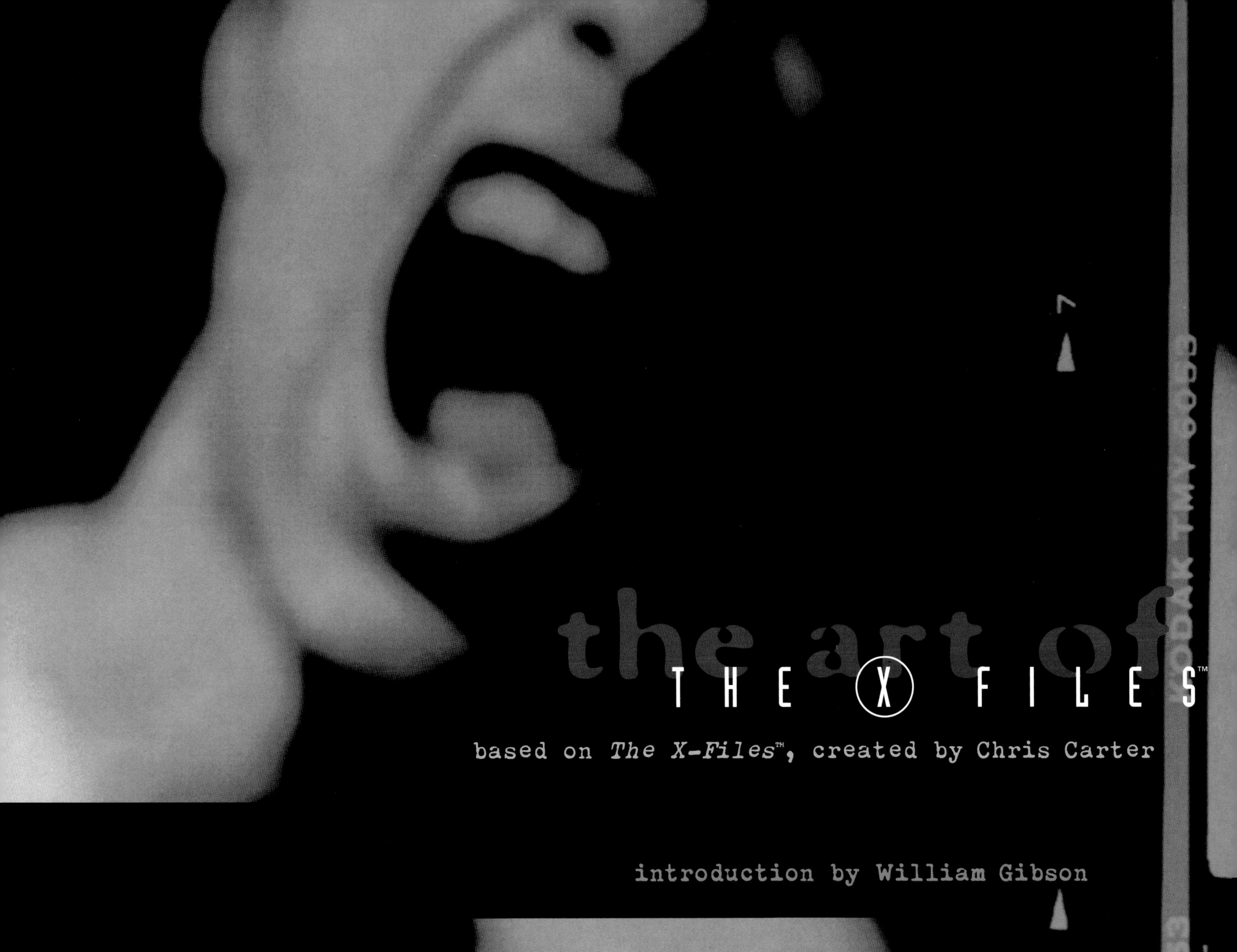

the art of THE X FILES™

based on *The X-Files*™, created by Chris Carter

introduction by William Gibson

Thom Ang
Richard Andre
Aziz + Cucher
John Baldessari
Mike Bidlo
Dike Blair
Gilles Chabannes
Bruce Charlesworth
Karen Cinorre
Eugene Clark
Barbara C. Crane
Gregory Crewdson
John de Fazio
Mark Dion
Tennessee Rice Dixon
Toni Dove

Jay Dunn
Nicole Eisenman
Jeanne C. Finley
Suzanne Fiol
Joy Garnett
Michelle Handelman &
Monte Cazazza
Lyle Ashton Harris
Julia Heyward
Brian Horton
Lisa A. Johnston
Joan Jonas
Bill Jones
Anne Marie Karlsen
Lisa Kereszi
Sean Kilcoyne

Komar & Melamid
Barbara Kruger
Paul Lamarre &
Melissa Wolf
Paul Lee
Minnette Lehmann
Rudy Lemcke
Robert Longo
Vera Lutter
Frank Majore
Aline Mare
Clay Patrick McBride
Larry Miller
John Monteith
Catherine Opie
Dennis Oppenheim

Marc Pally
Barbara Pollack
Daniel Reiser
David Robbins
David C. Scher
Julia Scher
John Schlesinger
Collier Schorr
Gerald Slota
Rose Stasuk
Robert Stivers
Oliver Wasow
Jill Waterman
Ken Weaver
Patty Wickman
Bruce & Norman Yonemoto

the artists

the absolute at large

William Gibson

Q: What do Canadian cities look like?

A: They look the way American cities do on televisions.

—pamphlet addressed to draft-evaders, Toronto, 1967

Welcome to the New World (dis)Order.

Welcome to ambient dread and a certain slippery ecstasy, a sensation akin to constantly walking on ball-bearings.

This is our "future," the one we didn't anticipate: call it Postmodernity.

The giddy anxiety we feel today has little to do with the millennium (another Christian holiday, so to speak) and much more to do with the end of Modernity. Many of us remain creatures of the Modern, more (increasingly) are creatures of the Postmodern, but the majority are still a bit of both.

We inhabit an unprecedentedly deep fault line of history; we are living amid changes so profound that we can only faintly apprehend them.

Civilization-as-we-know-it is ending.

Freud saw civilization, *kultur*, as being built upon a renunciation of primal urges. Civilized individuals exchanged some portion of the possibility of happiness for a measure of security. The costs of civilization, of Modernity, were suppression and regulation. In Postmodernity the swap reverses itself; we trade security for the scary and delirious possibilities of new happinesses, previously unthinkable gratifications.

Midcentury America was the heyday and homeland of Modernity: the future was out there, and in the official version at least, it was *all gain*. We were taught, in effect, that there could be gains without losses; that the future, like happiness, was perfectible.

Yet we lived in a climate of corrosive, technologically induced global fear: the fear of MAD (Mutual Assured Destruction) and nuclear winter. The mono-fear of the Cold War has gone now, redeployed into the fabric of an emergent order.

The X-Files is one of my favorite expressions of all of this.

The show is a chimera, a mutant; a final, brilliantly inbred expression of the Age of Broadcast Television. Like the two-headed dog it is, it manages both to bite the hand that feeds it *and* move phenomenal numbers of units. It is a seamless pop artifact. It is a disturbing and viscerally satisfying expression of where we've come from, where we are today, and all those places where we simultaneously yearn and dread to go. Chris Carter, its creator, is the New Auteur: a *re-curator* of the seething media-soup we swim in. His business, to borrow a phrase from Kingsley Amis, is the production of "new maps of hell."

The X-Files is not "about" conspiracy theories and the paranormal, so much as it is of the Postmodern. This is the Age of Deregulation, and in *The X-Files*, as in our daily lives, *the very nature of reality is deregulated*. Consensus-reality floats, like the dollar, the yen, and our destiny, in the irrational moral blindness of market forces.

Mulder and Scully are the quintessential Postmodern Couple, their relationship perfectly expressing the postmodern redeployment of sex (which

ould threaten rather than
eal their union). Religion,
n *The X-Files*, is entirely
ostmodern, its manifesta-
ions split between the
emi-humanist GOMU (God-
f-my-understanding) of
he Christian New Age and
he darkest extremes of
undamentalism (Jonestown,
he Christian heresy of
atanism).

This is, seriously, some
erious stuff, and entirely
orthy of being reflected
n franchise-objects of an
dgier sort than the usual
ontainer-ship mountains of
offee mugs, novelizations,
um-cards, and the like.

Hence this book, a col-
ection of images either
reated for or presented in
elation to *The X-Files*.
nother act of sampling, of
curation and re-curation.
Along with the "soundtrack"
CD, this is easily the
coolest and most appropri-
ate X-Files associational
item. Check out John
Baldessari's *Goya Series: I
Saw It, 1997*; redeployed
from its Serious Art con-
text, it suggests the work
of some white-shirted CIA
drone up for weeks on mag-
nesium pemoline, the walls
of his McLean cubicle
lined with images of the
Absolute. Or Mark Dion's
Untitled, a 760-pound mole
strung up in another sort
of cubicle, this one imagined in the endlessly plastic postreal nonspace of
PhotoShop. Or (for myself
the most haunting
of all) Oliver Wasow's
Untitled #313, in which
Something erupts beyond
swan and windowlight,
beneath a Turneresque,
television sky.

This is, if you will, a
poetic response to a show
whose deepest meanings are
more interestingly bent,
more deeply subversive
than any dream of a gray
and covert They expressed
therein. These artists are
connecting directly with
something deeply strange—
the very thing Mr. Carter
and his minions connect
with. They have seen that
which is even now abduct-
ing us, and it is us.

See it with them. Enjoy.

THE TRUTH IS OUT THERE

The Expulsion from Paradise (The Original X-File), **Thom Ang**

HTP-197.04.10
CONFIDENTIAL ITEMS OF A HIGHLY SENSITIVE NATURE. HANDLE EXPEDITIOUSLY ON A STRICTLY NEED-TO-KNOW BASIS VIA SECURE CHANNELS. NOTICE: ANYONE WHO UNLAWFULLY DISCLOSES, REMOVES, MUTILATES, DESTROYS, OR REPRODUCES ANY ITEM FROM THIS FILE WILL BE PROSECUTED TO THE FULLEST EXTENT OF LOCAL, STATE, AND FEDERAL LAWS. © ANDRE 1997

AI-UNIT | BI-UNIT | CI-UNIT | FI-UNIT

Richard Andre ARTIST NAME: R.E.A

© RICHARD ANDRE, NYC, APR '97

HTP-197.04.10
INK ON 100% COTTON PAPER;
BLOOD, BONE MARROW, & SKIN ON GLASS
IN ARCHIVAL EVIDENCE SLEEVES & FILE.
11 7/8 x 17 15/16 INCHES (30.1 x 46.3 cm)

HTP-197.04.10, Richard Andre

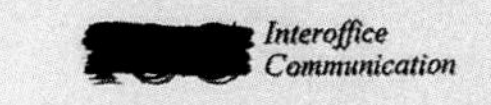

CONFIDENTIAL

Interoffice Communication

TO

FROM

SUBJECT **HTP-197.04.10**

Recent events indicate scientists and doctors involved in the ████████ might be reluctant to work with our foreign friends. To ensure this reluctance does not develop into an intra-project resistance, this office recommends that the EOC establish a task force to stabilize relations (see Roster printed below and Unit Files attached hereto).

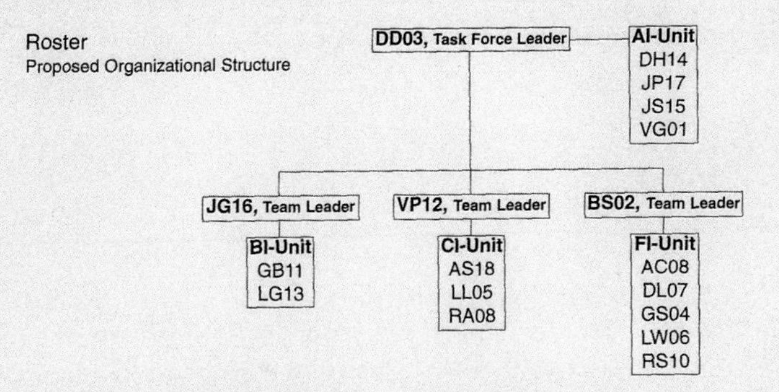

The proposed task force has been partially briefed and is completely capable of carrying out the mission as previously outlined by the EOC which would involve contact with our foreign friends. A HTP candidate has been selected to closely assist our friends in their research. This office submits the candidate's blood, bone marrow, and skin samples to the EOC for DNA compatibility testing (see Slides at right).

This office is confident that HTP members challenged by the history, ethics and moral character of our foreign friends are more likely to reconcile their differences once the proposed task force is in place. This office urges the EOC to establish and implement the proposed task force to safeguard against potential disruption of the ████████ mission to assist the direction of natural selection and human evolution.

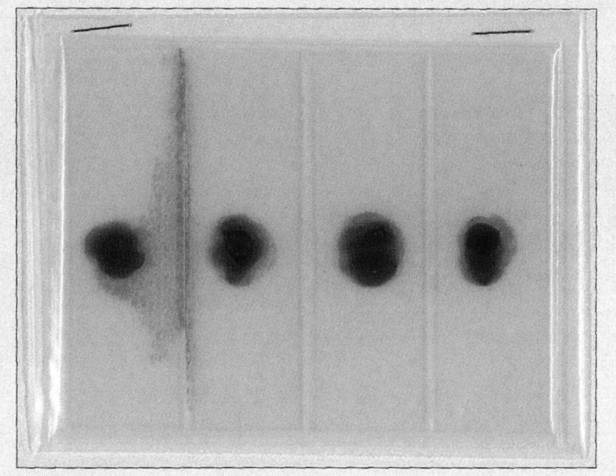

BLOOD SAMPLES, 1-5

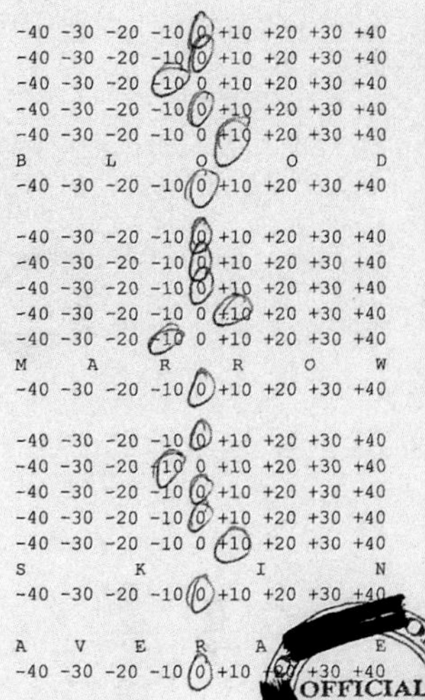

DNA FIELD TEST RESULTS

BONE MARROW SAMPLES, 1-5

SKIN SAMPLES, 1-5

HTP-197.04.10

the Truth, somewhere out there.

 Untitled (After Man Ray), **Aziz + Cucher**

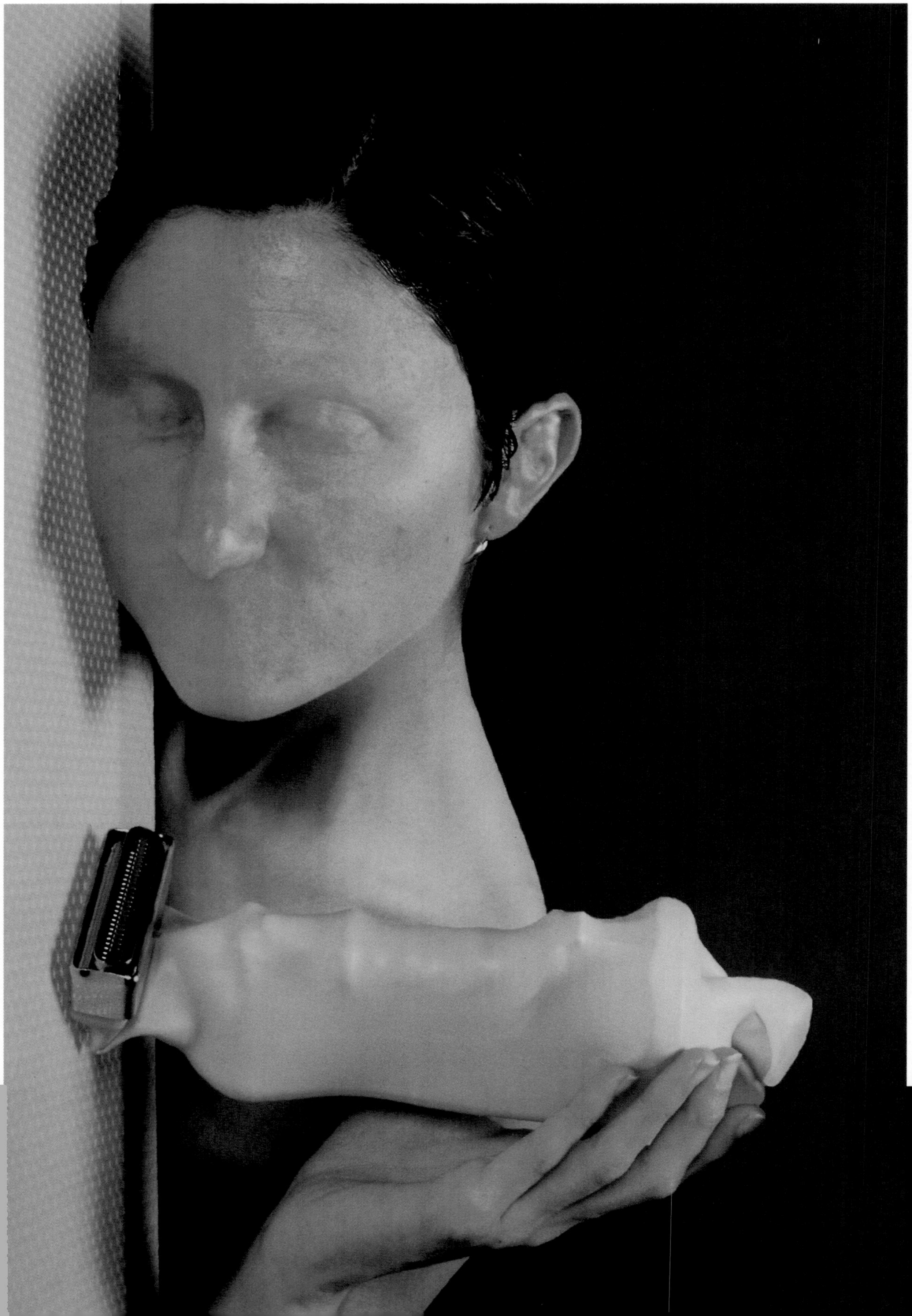

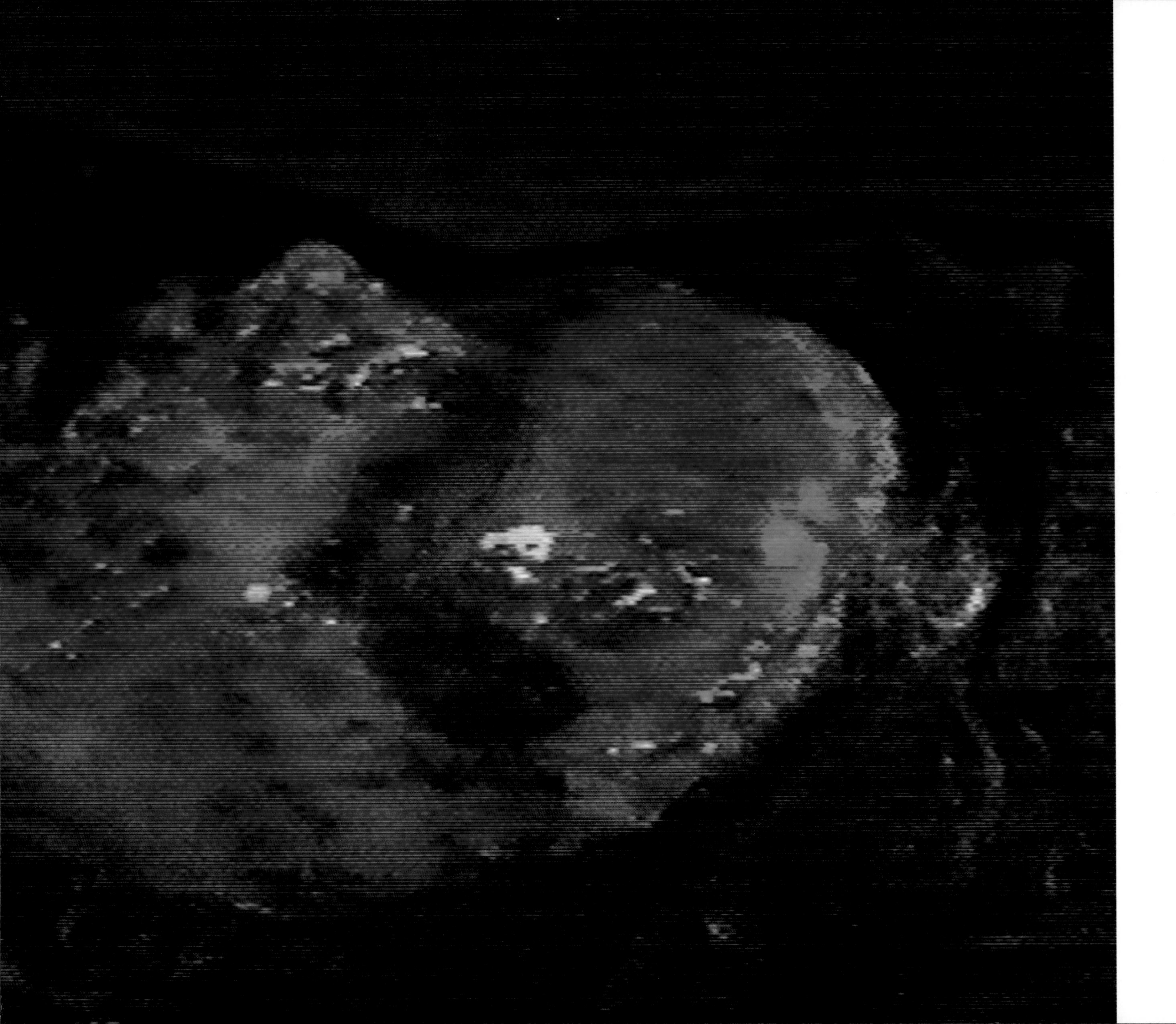

AF Captures Flying

Ranch in Roswell

I SAW IT

Goya Series: I Saw It, **John Baldessari**

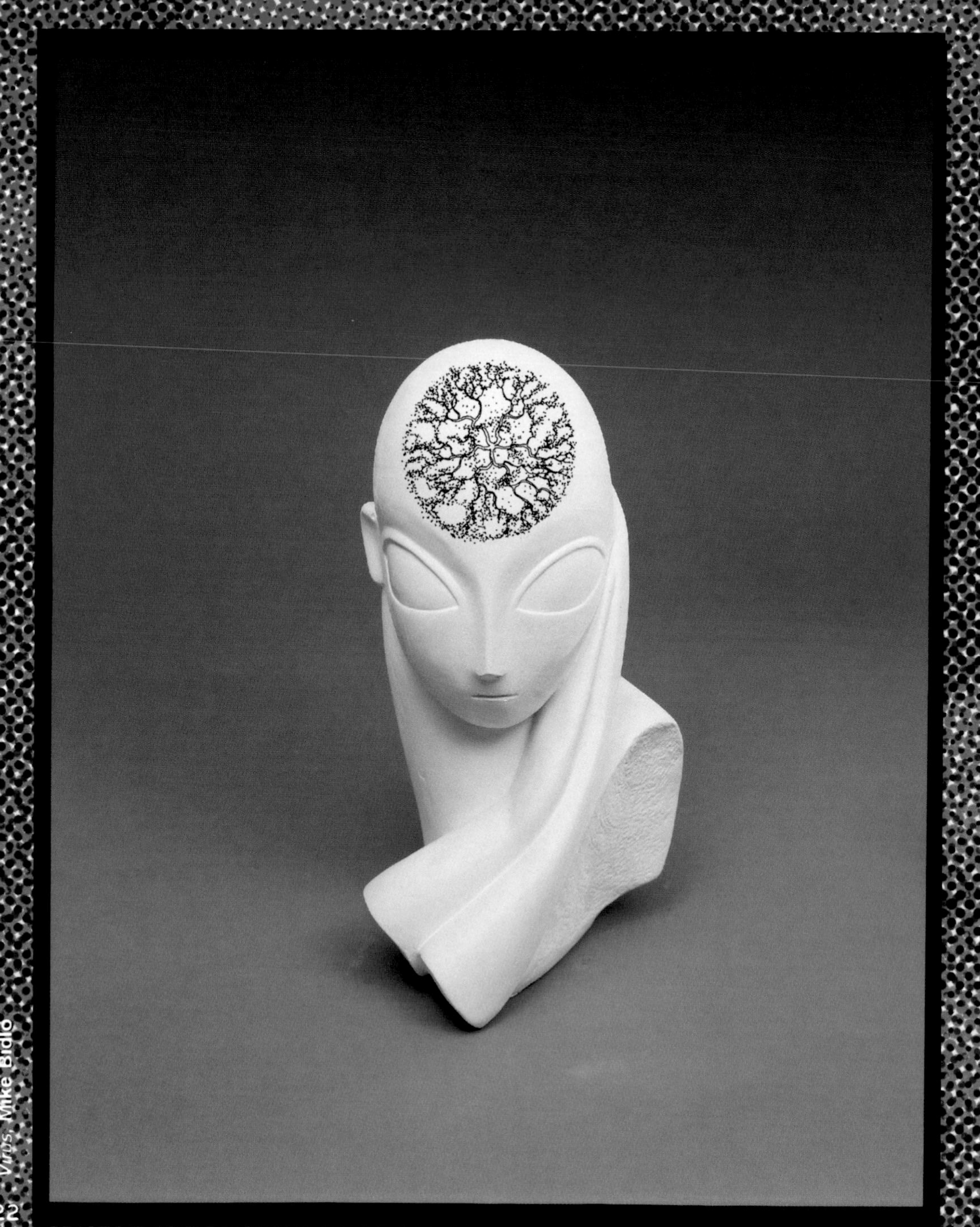

Virus, Mike Bidlo

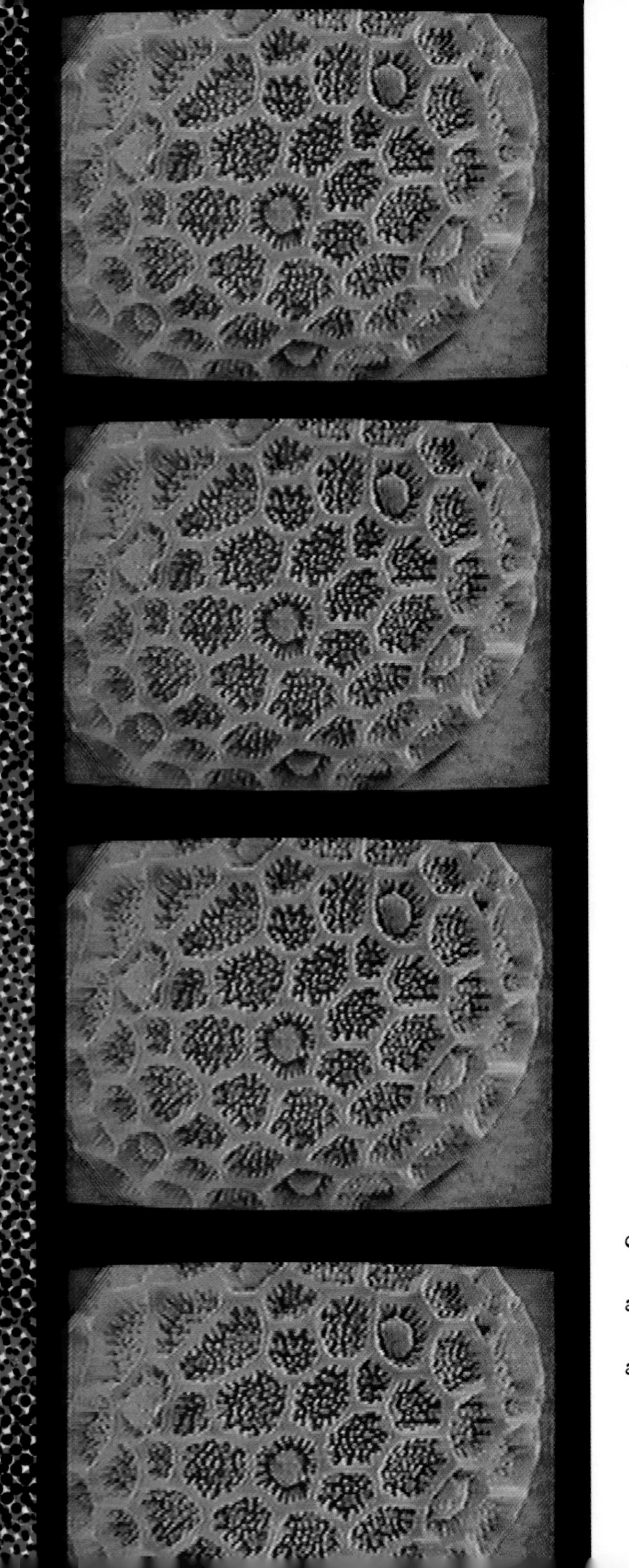

This "choice" was based on a reaction of visual indifference and a total absence of good or bad taste...in fact, a complete anesthesia.

ast of extremely [illegible]
ugh the forward wi[illegible]
s if searching for [illegible]
s Fenig's row. He is frozen

t shines
en moves
. The light
n his seat.

I love looking at *The X-Files* for its places and things; airports, ashtrays, cell phones, flashlights, hospitals, Marlboros, motels, and rent-a-cars.

Untitled, **Dike Blair**

Ezekiel: Tech Angel, **Gilles Chabannes**

A semifamous architect once said that four forces were struggling for world domination: art, religion, science, and insanity. I consider insanity a category equivalent to "miscellaneous" or "irrational." *The X-Files* is a prime candidate for this "miscellaneous" worldview. The show directly challenges science, while remaining within an interesting amalgam of urban myths and secular mysteries.

My piece illustrates, in parable form, what I consider to be the central theme of the series. *Ezekiel: Tech Angel* is a high-tech inversion of the expulsion from the Garden of Eden. A forbidden, remote site (Roswell, Site 52), central to the narrative, is animated by apparitions of unexplained lights. The narrative is a subset of the Biblical end-of-the-world–apocalyptic story, complete with the arrival of the Archangel Michael and his angels in the form of bright UFOs.

Ezekiel refers to the Biblical Apparition mentioned in the Book of the Prophets: *Ezekiel* and *Tech Angel* is a contemporary reference, with a wink at the famous pop song "Teen Angel."

My interest in *The X-Files* has less to do with monsters and spacemen than with the ways the show depicts ordinary things. The weekly accumulation of particular objects, places, and people is designed to trigger associations that can outstrip any simulated horror. Fear springs from realistic human conflict on this show and is revved up by dark shadows. Many more of the literally rendered paranormal sequences are defined as viewpoints, dreams, or meditations. This ploy allows any character's theory or hallucination to be visualized, freeing the show to welcome all manner of subjects, genres, and modes of expression—including comedy. This open aspect is what sustains *The X-Files* for me. So is the absence of vampires. I hate those guys.

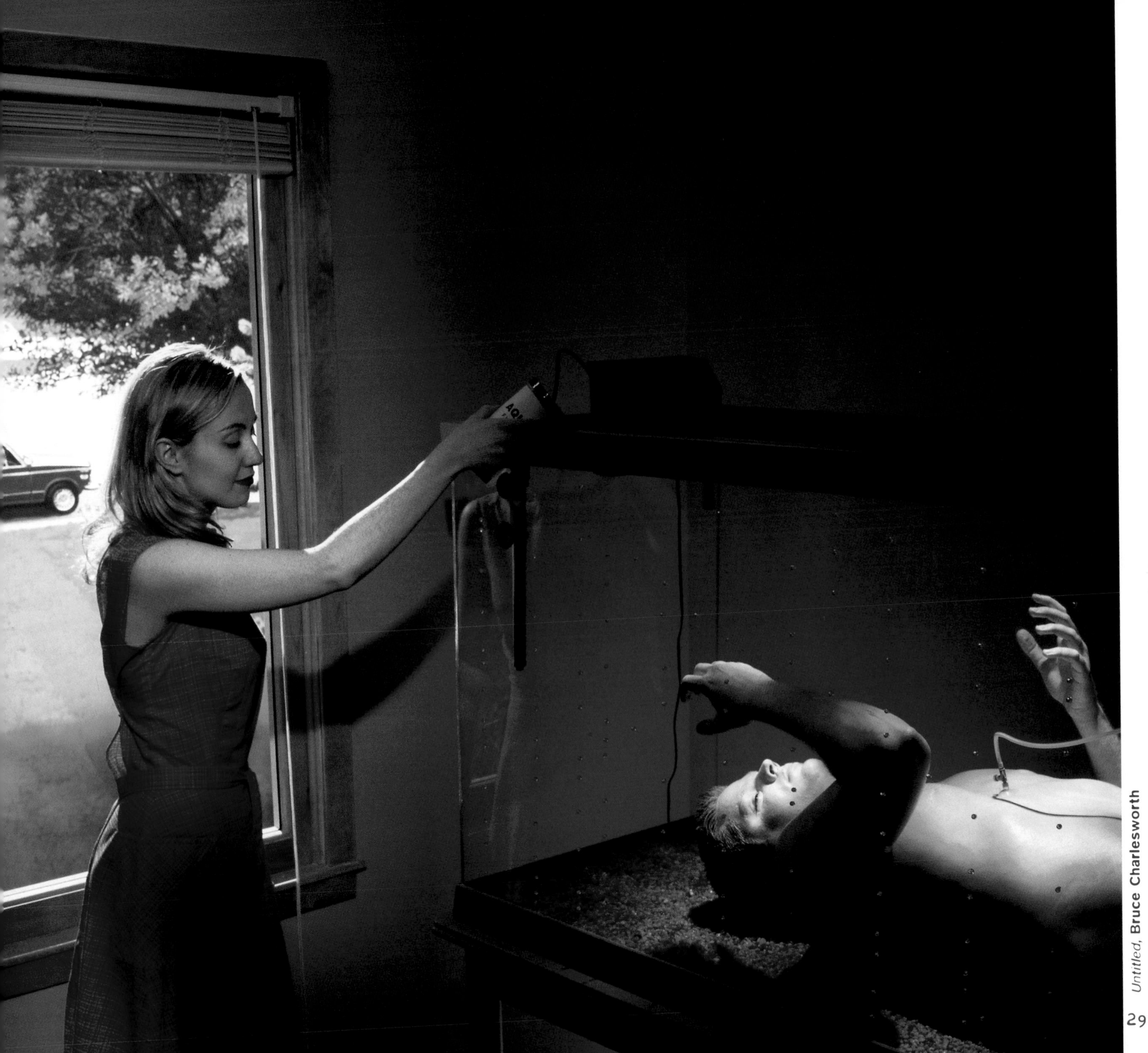

Untitled, **Bruce Charlesworth**

Still from "Toxic Shock", **Karen Cinorre**

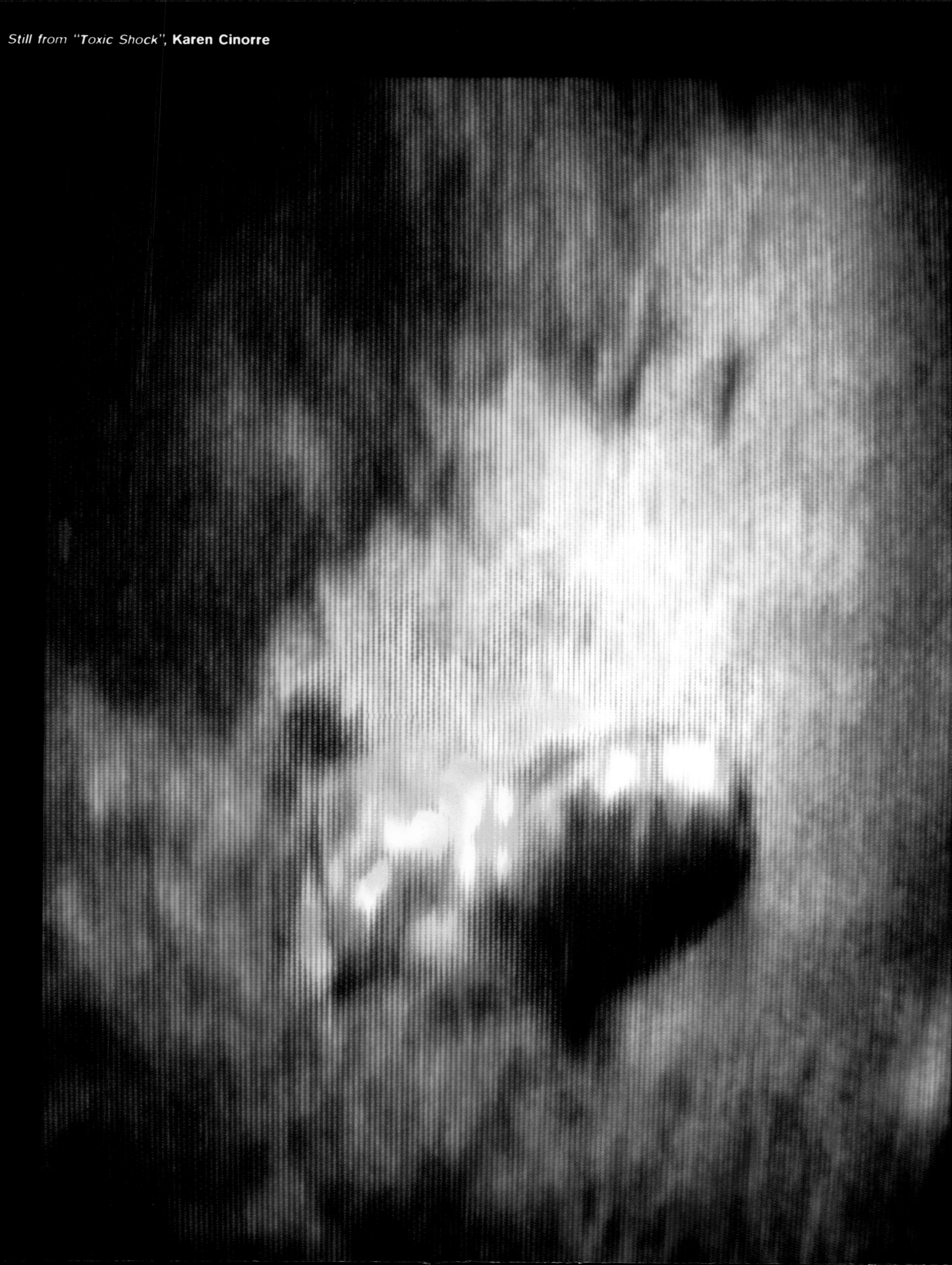

The X-Files is a source of inspira-

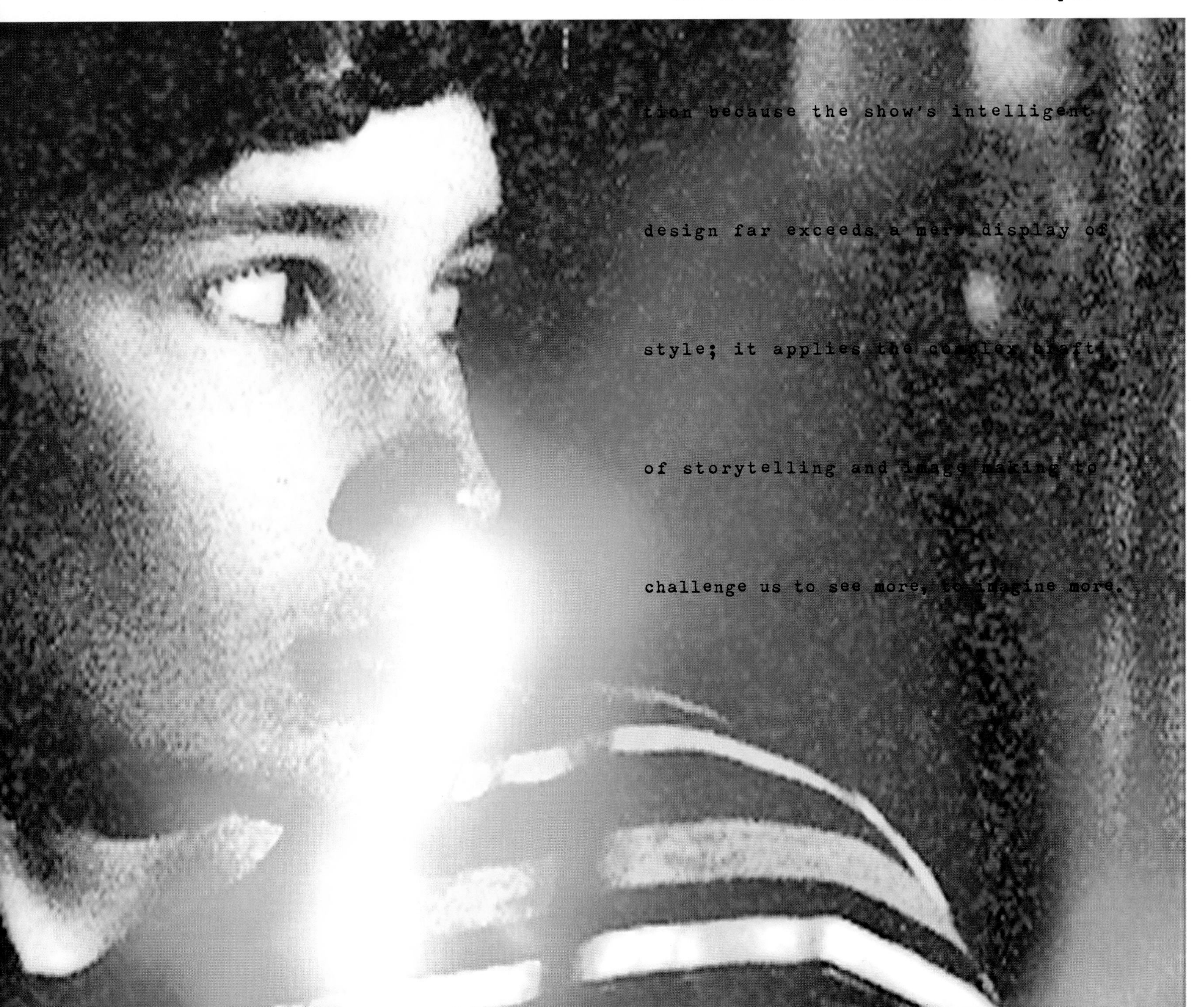

tion because the show's intelligent design far exceeds a mere display of style; it applies the complex craft of storytelling and image making to challenge us to see more, to imagine more.

I document the sites of supernatural happenings. These may take place in any number of locations, such as basements of small, secluded churches in rural areas. A pixel-vision, black-and-white video camera is the perfect tool to capture this raw data. Because of their semifused appearance, black-and-white video prints conjure up mysterious and elusive imagery. My three video prints capture essential elements of postabduction. The left video print reveals a fragment of the victim's semi-recognizable face, yet its mouth looks almost peaceful, as if all life were taken away before the victim had time to even consider death as an option. The second video print is of a gloved hand, protected so as not to expose its flesh to unknown substances, for fear of a close encounter with an undetectable bacteria. The third video print describes the debris of this postabduction scene, viewed as remains left behind from a disturbance we classify as a phenomenon. Standing behind the camera, splicing together a mysterious happening, almost confuses what I know as fantasy and reality. This is not merely TV viewing from my living room Lazyboy. I've submerged my subconscious into the world of the strange, not knowing if I will be able to get back, but then that may be the appeal.

Postabduction: Mouth, Glove, Debris, **Eugene Clark**

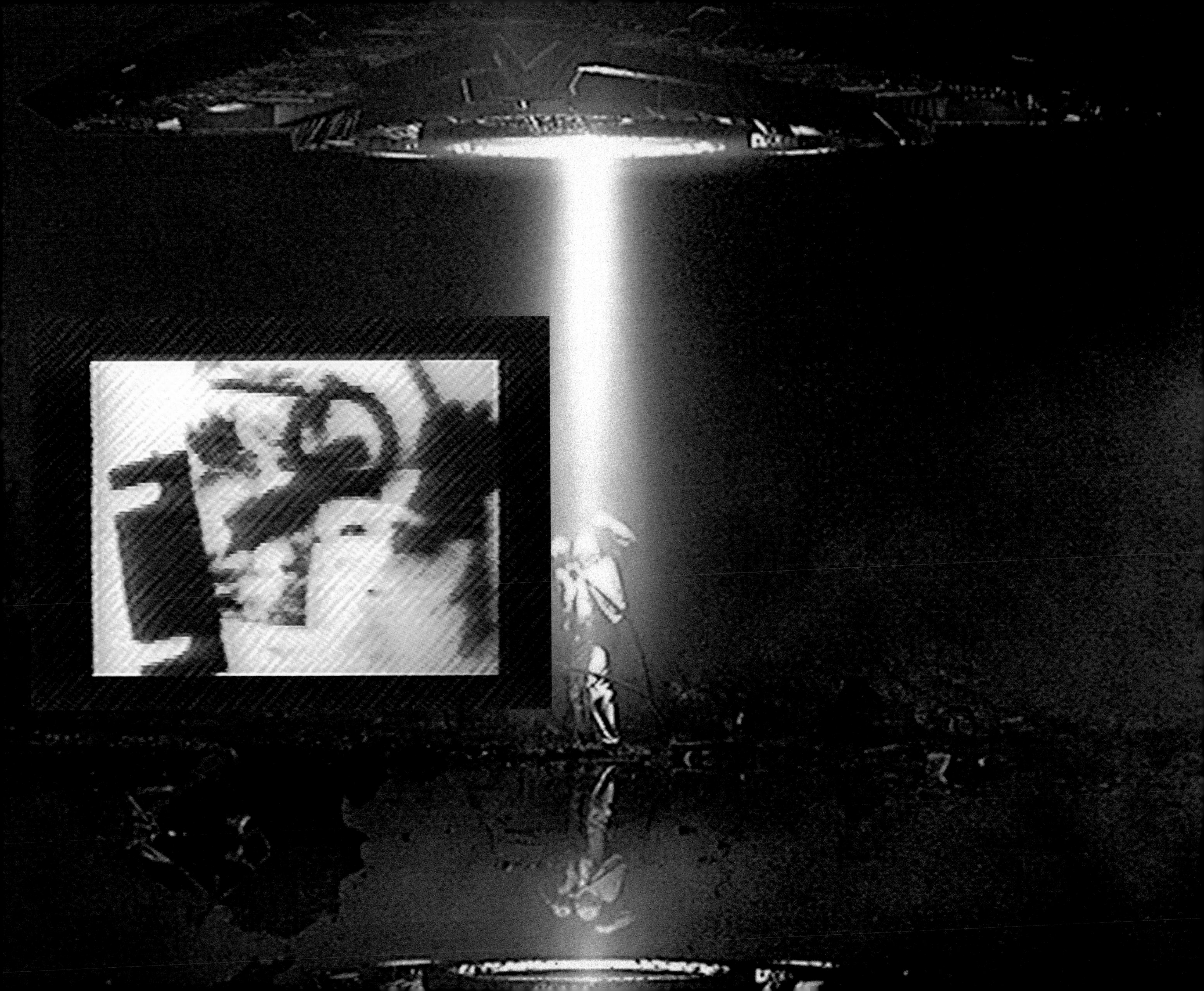

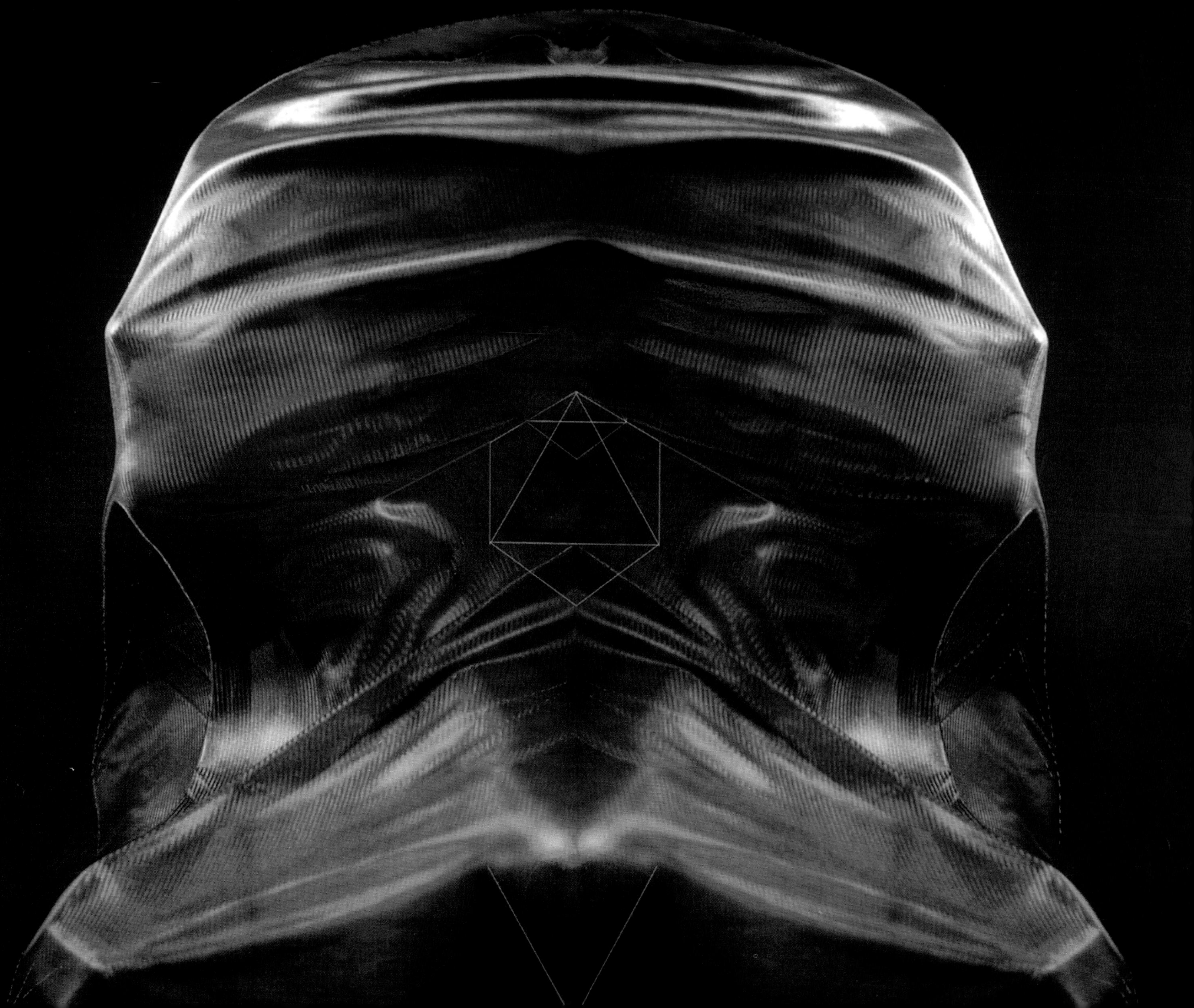

Doppelganger, **Barbara C. Crane**

To me, *The X-Files* is a fascinating metaphor for the workings of the mind. I see it dealing with the struggle between the unconscious mind that "knows" and the conscious mind that tries to "understand." Agent Mulder works on intuition and Agent Scully tries to be rational and objective.

Like my conscious mind, Scully is finally persuaded by her partner's evidence and must play the intermediary between Mulder and the "System." The "System" or the superego is deeply threatened by Mulder, whose revelations would certainly destabilize the false sense of security it is continuously manufacturing. Consequently his findings are suppressed and obscured. The cover-up is also hidden, creating a layering of inexplicable mysteries.

I am fascinated by the relationship between that which is half sensed, captured in the corner of one's eye, seen peripherally and therefore "known," and that which is in the conscious mind. I create images that are mirrors reflecting to the world what my unconscious mind senses. These images, like encapsulated dreams, can contain code or script, archetypal symbols, geometry, photographs, and paint. They are layered and veiled like *The X-Files*.

"TRUST NO ONE"

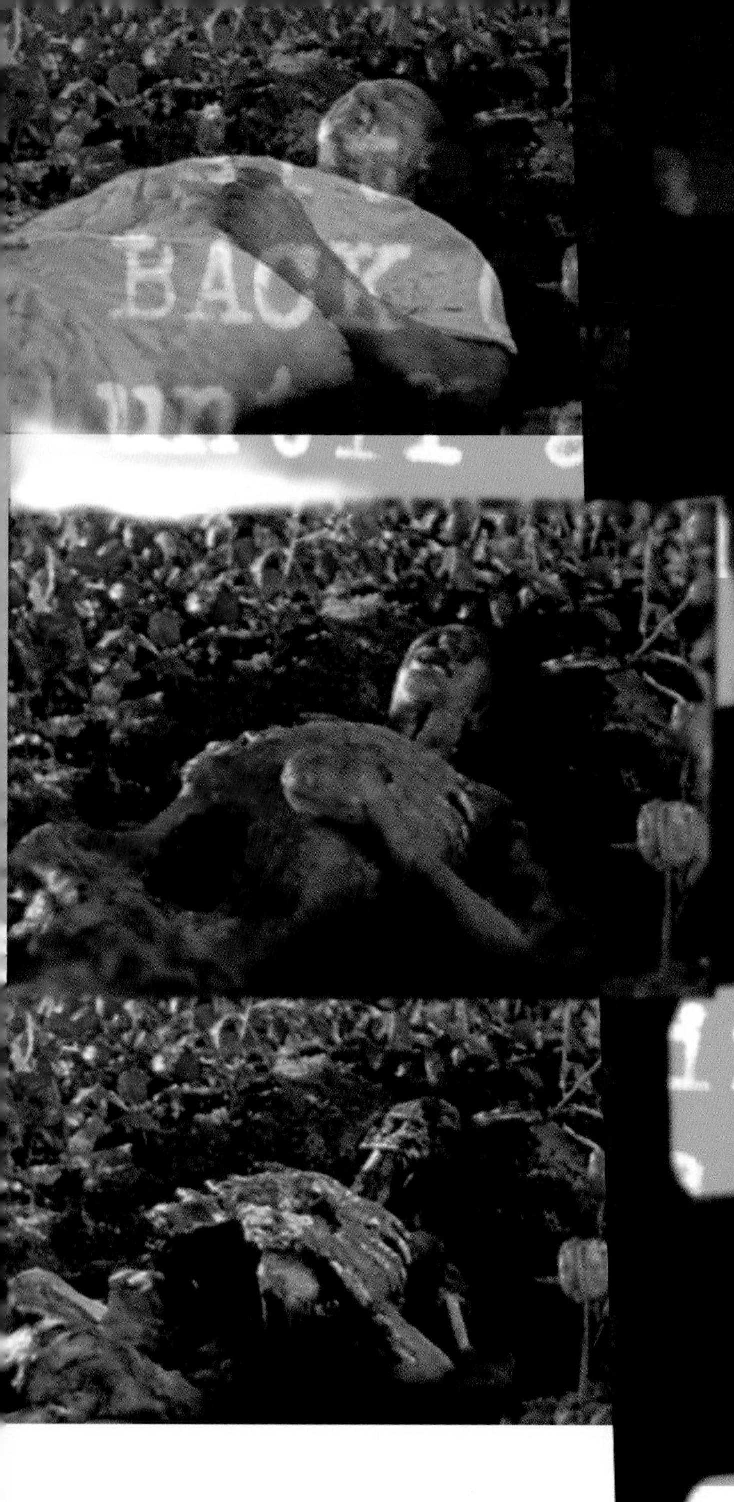

My elaborately staged tableaux of scenes in suburban backyards and gardens explore the domestic landscape and its relationship to the natural world. The highly detailed, large-scale dioramas obsessively recreate and enlarge upon the small dramatic events that occur within this familiar setting. My photographs do not picture the house and garden as a place of comfort and stability. Instead, they search beneath the veneer of domestic trappings to uncover a lurking sense of disquiet. These highly orchestrated photographs combine a disorienting pictorial scale with exaggerations in color and lighting to make ordinary scenes appear extraordinary and fantastic. This collision between the normal and the paranormal produces an uncanny tension that serves to transform the topology of the suburban landscape into a place of wonder and activity.

Within the parameters of my fictive landscapes, incidental scenes and occurrences—like a towering dirt pile, a circular formation of robin eggs, and an excavated hole in the ground—have the mystery and poetic resonance of a ritualistic site or private totem. It is as if these unnatural arrangements and disturbances contain unknowable secrets and alien knowledge. The significance of these enigmatic sites is never fully revealed, their complete stories and exact meanings remain unanswerable questions.

In this work, the security of the backyard is pushed further into the distance. The narrative events unfold along the selvages between yard and unmanicured perimeter. This borderland is transformed into a dark and hallucinatory forest of secrets, where increasingly fantastic and macabre scenes reveal a nature of impossible beauty, abundance, and decay.

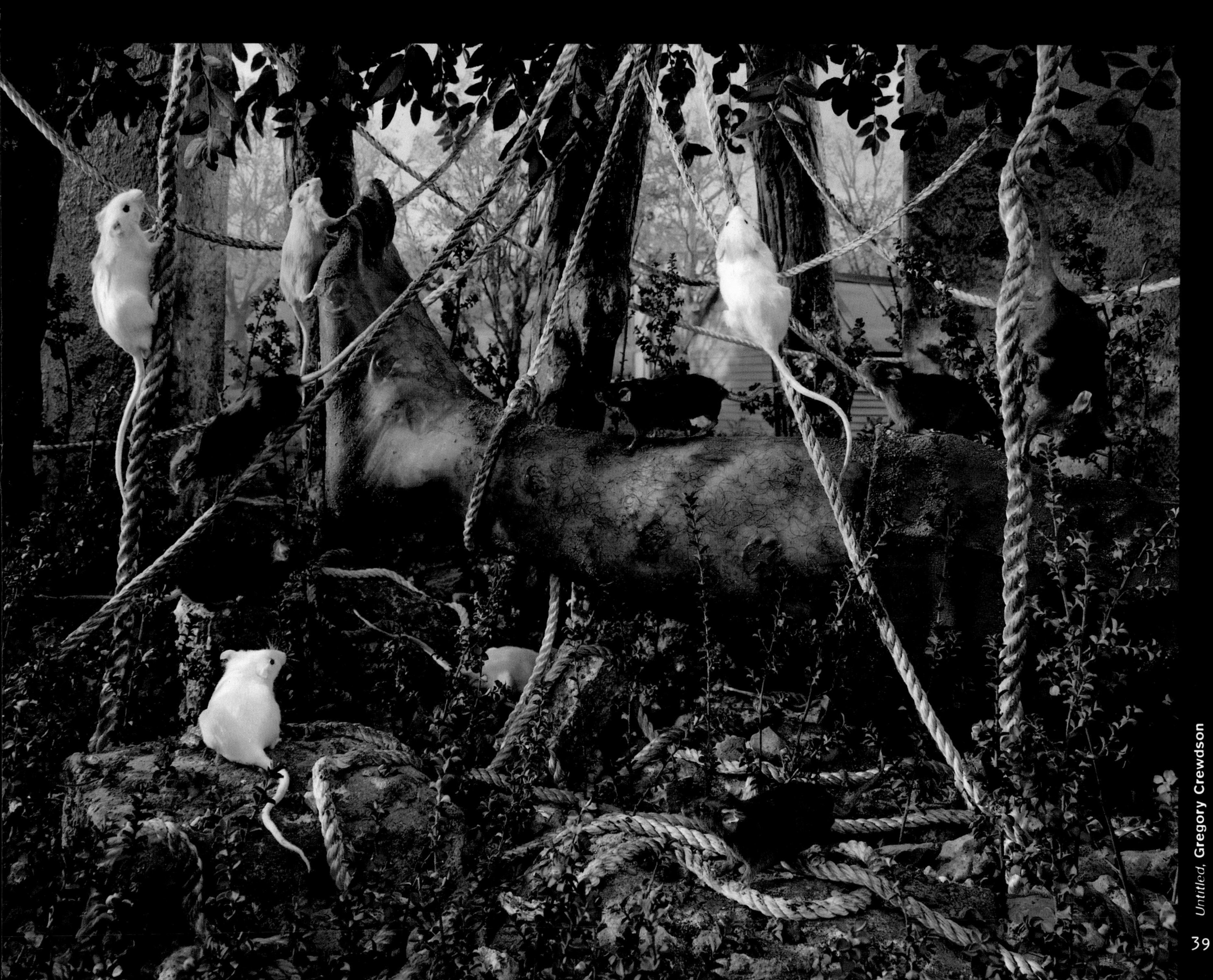

Untitled, **Gregory Crewdson**

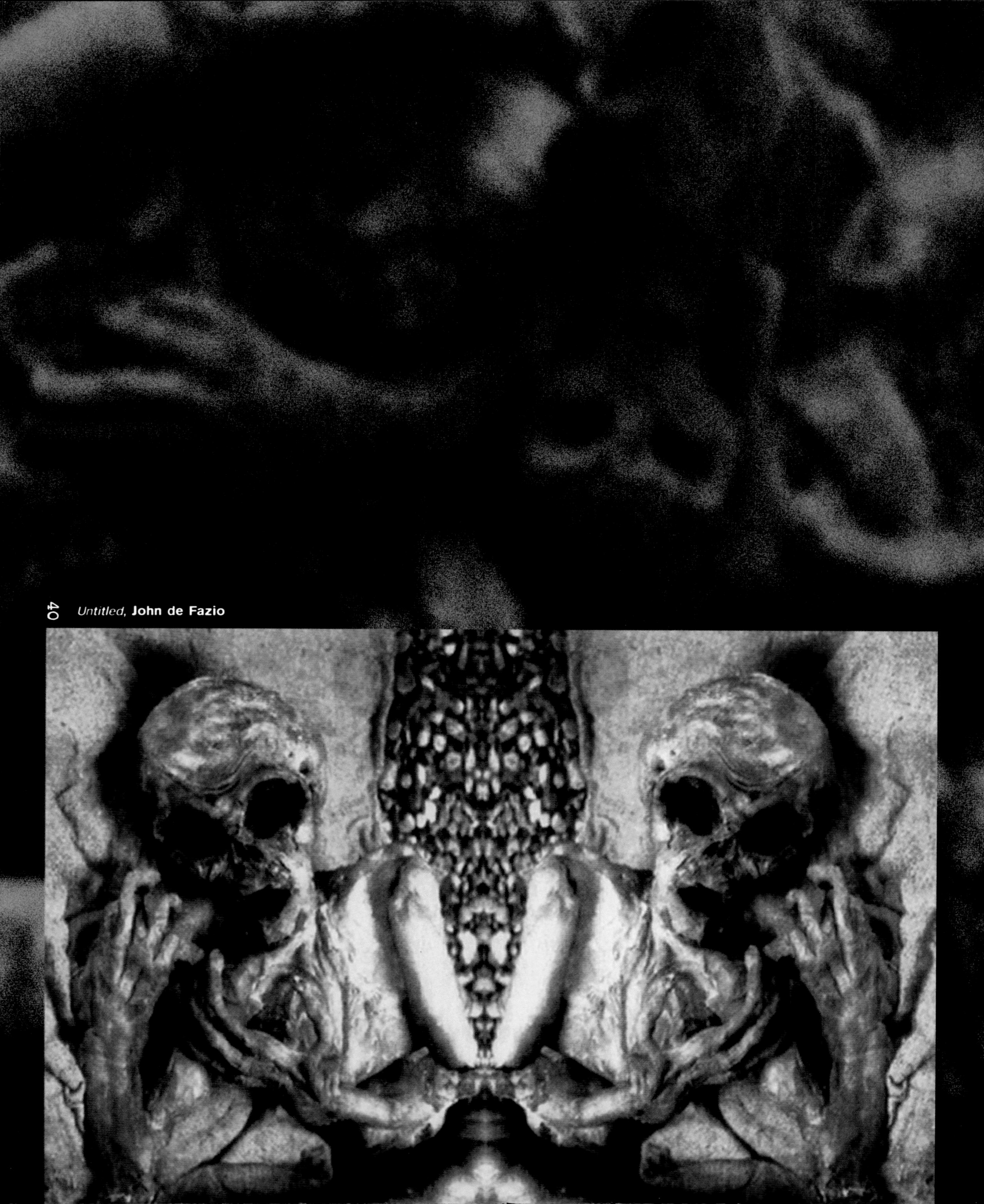

Untitled, **John de Fazio**

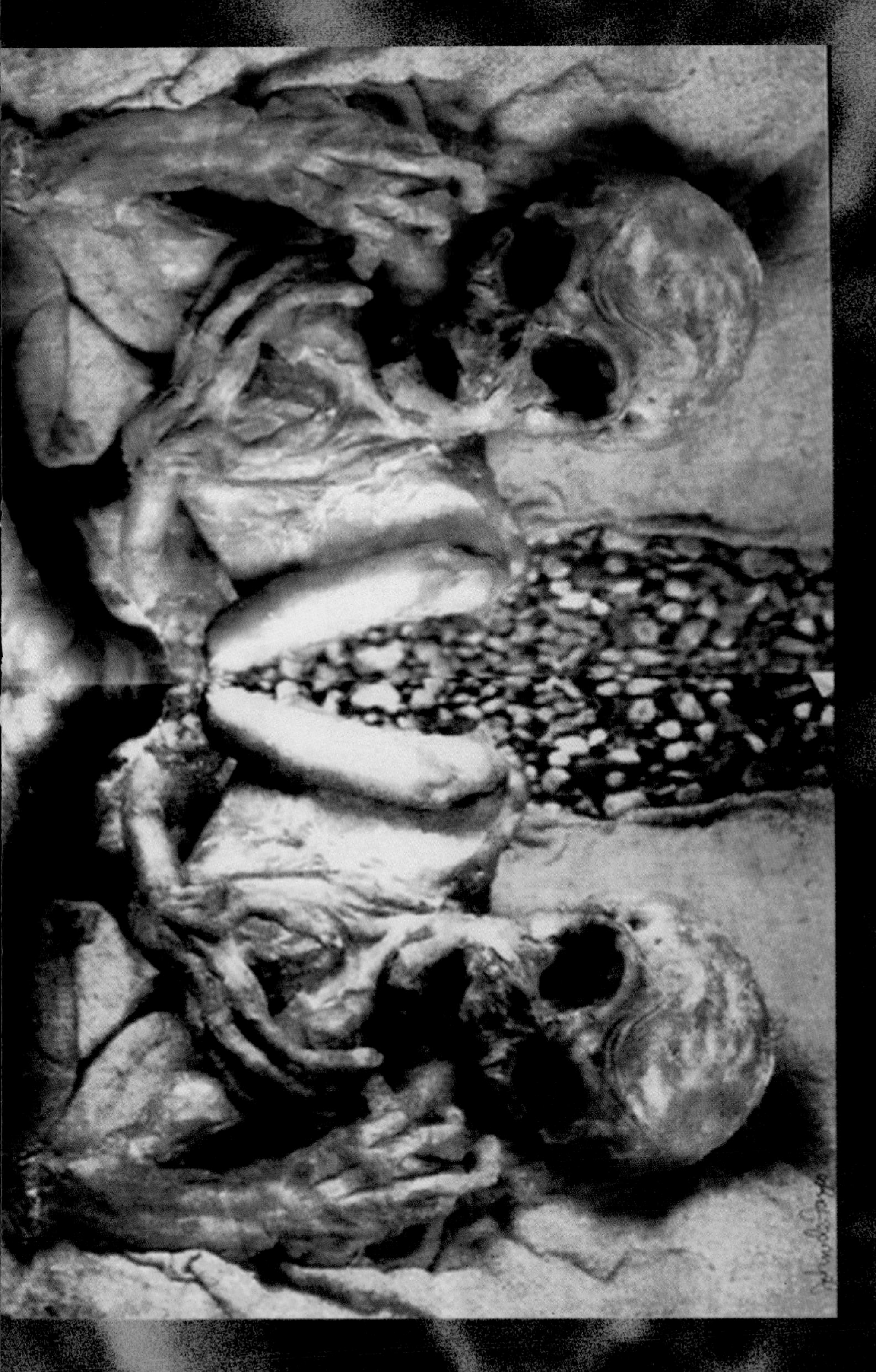

Sampling from the diverse selection of *The X-Files* mythologies, I was most attracted to an image of an alien corpse frozen in the throes of death. Dealing with reliquary in my previous work, I wanted to create an iconic image of the dead spaceman as twenty-first century savior, crash landing on Earth, his alien anatomy echoing our own mummified ancestors. By reduplicating this cosmic scream, I stumbled upon a kind of Rorschach test, reflecting our insatiable desire to see further signs of a universal connection with the Other.

There are two aspects of *The X-Files* that are wholly engrossing. First, *The X-Files* articulates a need, in an increasingly secularized society, for the construction of a coherent mythology. Like most mythologies, it places the fate of humanity in the hands of unseen supernatural forces. The alien hysteria in North America can be seen as a phenomenon fulfilling social needs akin to the classical pantheism, the Judeo-Christian tradition, and numerous other superstitions, religions, and folklores, past and present.

The second interesting feature of *The X-Files* is its deep-seated mistrust for conventional political authority. Most Americans know only too well that we live in a plutocracy rather than a legitimate democracy. In other words, we live in a situation in which the government is run by a wealthy, elite political class. *The X-Files* responds not only to the predictable abuse of authority such a system encourages, but to the frustration of people who feel alienated from the decision making process of their own government. Trust no one.

The X-Files, like many forms of the sci-fi or horror genre, functions as dreams for individuals, a safe place to resolve deeply disturbing daily anxieties.

What I find inspiring about *The X-Files* for my own work (beyond the sheer pleasure of its intelligence) is its ability to find the remarkable and the macabre in the everyday. This is a quality I also enjoyed about the *Night Stalkers* series from my childhood.

I am the Chupacabra

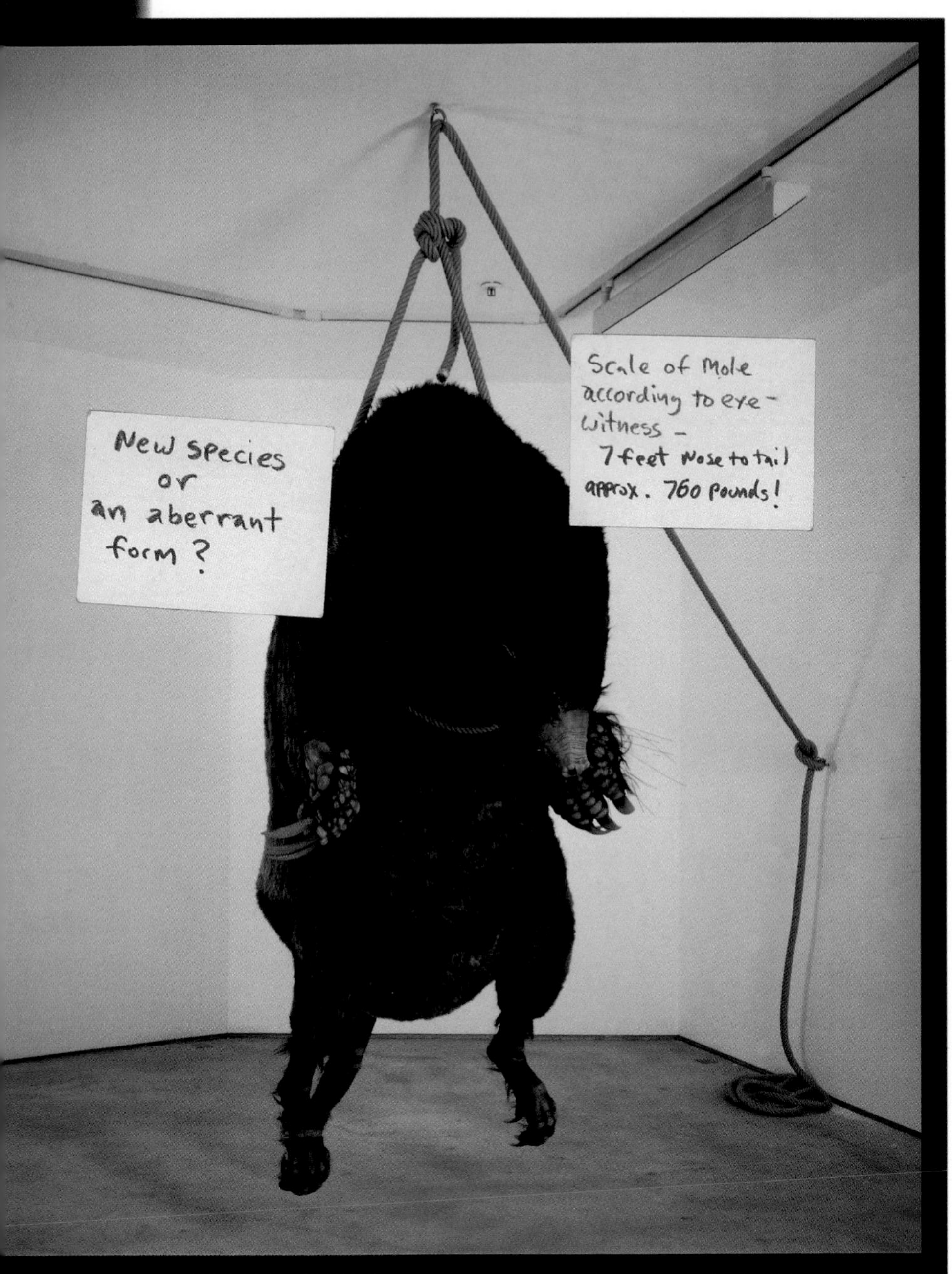

Untitled, **Mark Dion**

The common ground between *The X-Files* and my own work are the idiosyncratic dark stories with overlapping realities, the mix of unconscious and spiritual realms with scientific and rational procedures, arcane traditions intersecting mainstream, and high-tech knowledge. Stories in which eerie shadow forces and arche-types erupt into everyday life, manifest in physical form or psychological conflict, and must be contended with by ordinary people.

gly
aches
ead

Who is this woman, both a voice and a chorus? Zilith sings her song, a chain of fluid identities, multiple and partial, simultaneous and disseminate.The terrifying, formless, chaos of flesh is escalated and displaced. She acts out her resistance, telegraphing herself along the nodes of the Link. Unstable cracks and fissures appear in the psychic somatic field, the sky fluttering orifices are like windows onto a space we can't yet see. She sings strange sounds and the Link hums, vibrating with its traveling waves against the blood red sky.

The screen was never so dark on the TV before *The X-Files* and that was the first surprise. The continuing surprise was the mix of *Dragnet* and pulp genre fiction to create an undercurrent of content that speaks to cultural anxieties as if they're a cartoon sci-fi serial. I'm particularly interested in the capacity of genre fiction to create allegory. *Alice in Wonderland* is a critique of monarchy, H. G. Wells's *War of the Worlds* is an examination of colonialism, and *The Wind in the Willows* is an analysis of class relations.

Zilith crept quietly into the underground chamber, peering into the darkness to be certain she was alone and undetected. She feels manipulated by forces she can't find. The corporation—a gas, a spirit—is everywhere, permeating everything and yet nowhere. What to blow up? Where was the enemy? No matter presented itself—no center, no target. Cryptography is the new munition, she thought, public keys and secret keys—codes of access and their gates. She is hacking routers—taking over data paths and passing through gates by decrypting secret keys—to map the invisible loci of power. A researcher of distribution in the information market—a virtual urban planner from the informal sector.

From *Artificial Changelings*, **Toni Dove**

ÉÍ ’AANÍÍGÓÓ ’ÁHOOT’É

emembrance upon waking and the dream itself. *The X-Files* creates an osphere in which all subjective truth, however unlikely, can be consid-d objectively possible: in this willingness to be open minded, we share mon ground.

Deception Bay Worldwide: two stills from "The Messenger", **Jay Dunn**

Untitled, **Nicole Eisenman**

Time Bomb, **Jeanne C. Finley,** drawn from the videotape *Time Bomb* by Jeanne C. Finley and John Muse

"So here and there on my coverlet lie lost things out of my childhood and are as new. All forgotten fears are there again.

The fear that a small, woolen thread that sticks out of the hem of my blanket may be hard and sharp like a steel needle; the fear that this crumb of bread now falling from my bed may arrive glassy and shattered on the floor; the fear that some number may begin to grow in my brain until there is no more room for it inside me; the fear that I may betray myself and tell all that I dread.

I asked for my childhood and it has come back, and I feel that it is just as difficult as it was before, and that it has been useless to grow older."

—Rainer Maria Rilke, *The Notebooks of Malte Laurids Brigge*

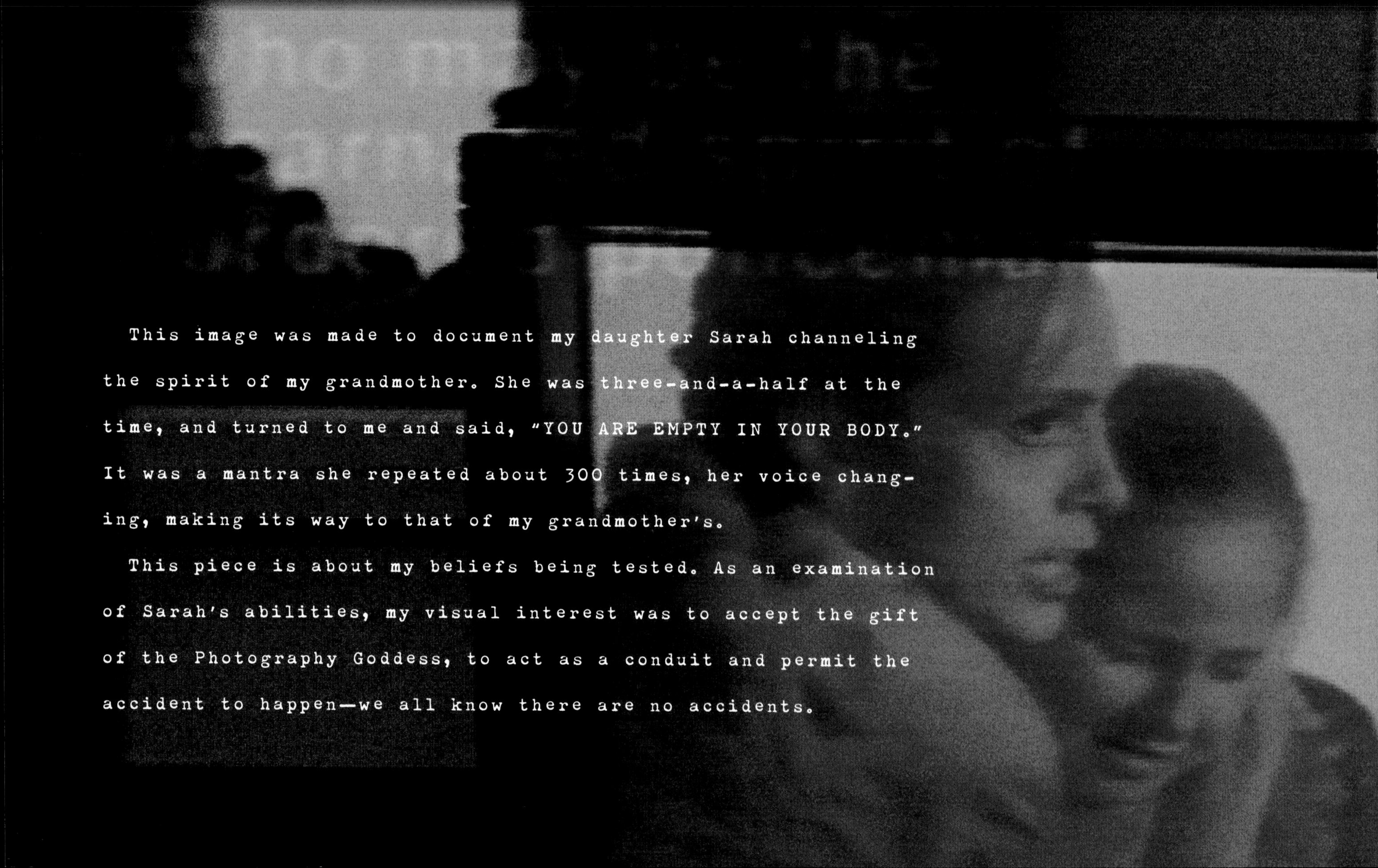

This image was made to document my daughter Sarah channeling the spirit of my grandmother. She was three-and-a-half at the time, and turned to me and said, "YOU ARE EMPTY IN YOUR BODY." It was a mantra she repeated about 300 times, her voice changing, making its way to that of my grandmother's.

This piece is about my beliefs being tested. As an examination of Sarah's abilities, my visual interest was to accept the gift of the Photography Goddess, to act as a conduit and permit the accident to happen—we all know there are no accidents.

 The Child Spirit—You Are Empty in Your Body, **Suzanne Fiol**

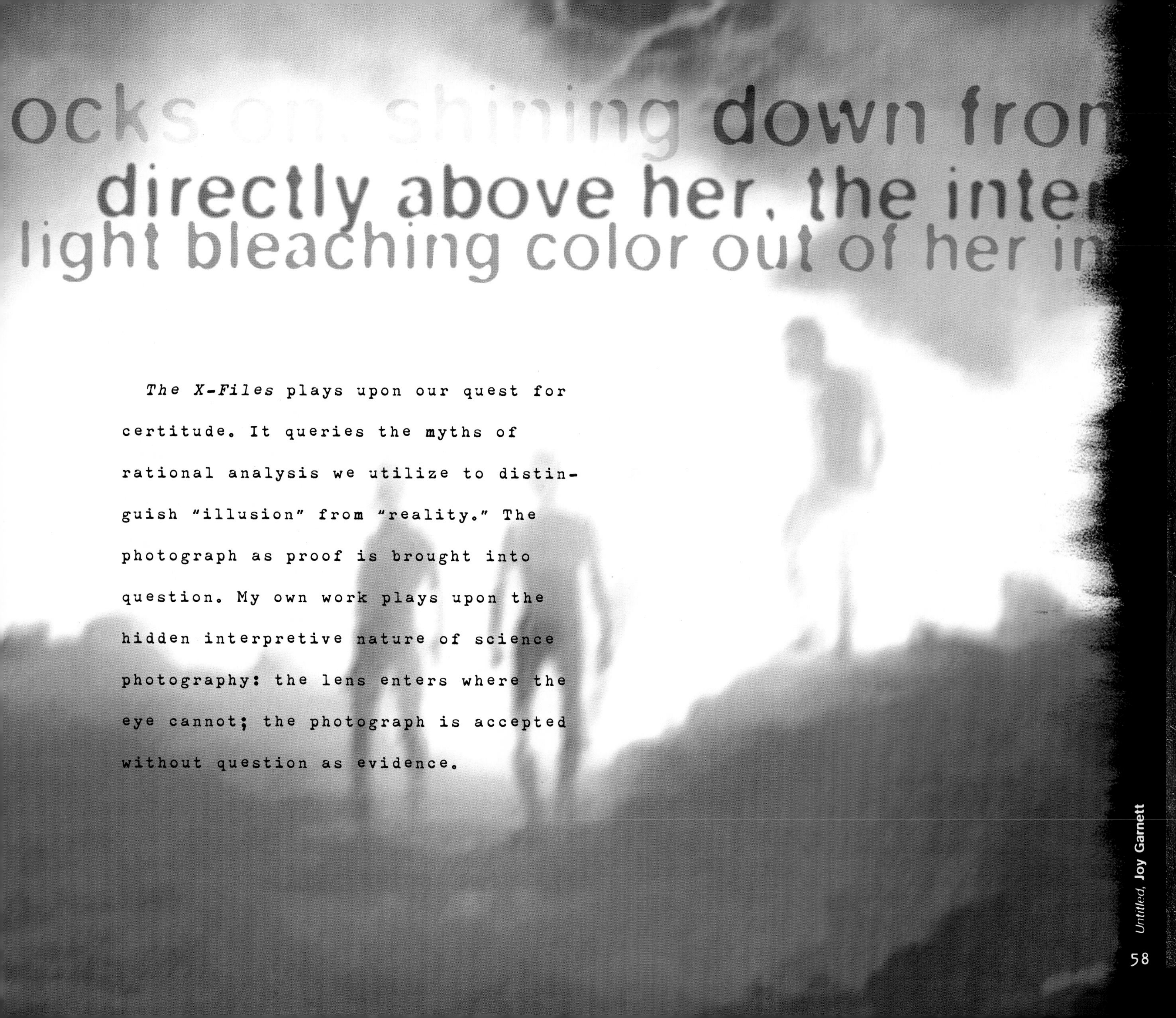

ocks on shining down fro
directly above her, the inte
light bleaching color out of her in

The X-Files plays upon our quest for certitude. It queries the myths of rational analysis we utilize to distinguish "illusion" from "reality." The photograph as proof is brought into question. My own work plays upon the hidden interpretive nature of science photography: the lens enters where the eye cannot; the photograph is accepted without question as evidence.

Untitled, **Joy Garnett**

APOLOGY IS POLICY

Untitled, from the series *Blood, Guts and Beauty*, **Michelle Handelman and Monte Cazazza**

A McLuhanesque police state where only the

paranoid survive. Paranormal paranoia because

what you know can kill you and probably will.

Xenophobic and Christlike, it links X to Y.

Trusting your television is like believing in

God...because what you don't know can kill you,

and probably will.

Paranoia is the highest state of consciousness.

—William S. Burroughs

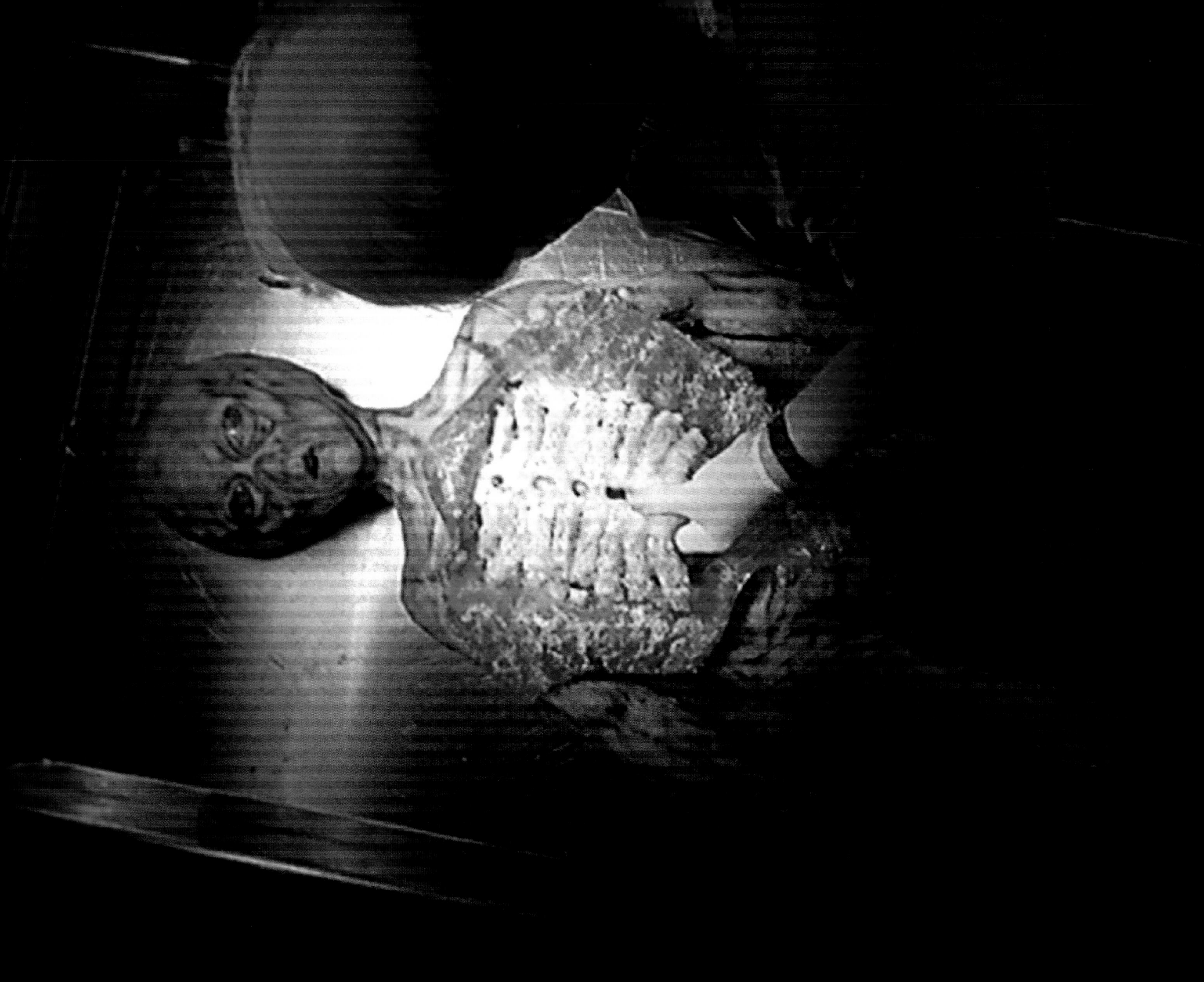

Untitled (use me), **Lyle Ashton Harris**

X666, **Julia Heyward**

What I like most about *The X-Files* is its treatment of popular mythology, especially concerning aliens. I like the tug-of-war dialectic between the believer Mulder and the skeptic Scully. My favorite show is the one in which the writers mix alien hybrid race mythology with the factual and atrocious German super-race experiments of the Second World War.

r nothing can seem foul to those that win."

Henry IV, Pt. 1 Act 5, Sc. 1

Sometimes the darkest secrets are the ones that we keep from ourselves.

PART 1

"Things really did go well in Dealey Plaza."

Tiny Secrets, **Brian Horton**

PART II

Just down the road aways from Graceland."

Treatise of Abduction, **Lisa A. Johnston**

"they
com

As a part of a new generation of artists who are exploring the boundaries of both fine arts and popular culture, I merge an appreciation for the photographic arts with an affinity for advanced digital imagery and computer technology. Challenging standards, while adhering to principles and investigating possibilities, is the essence of art and life.

EVERYTHING DIES

Untitled, **Joan Jonas**

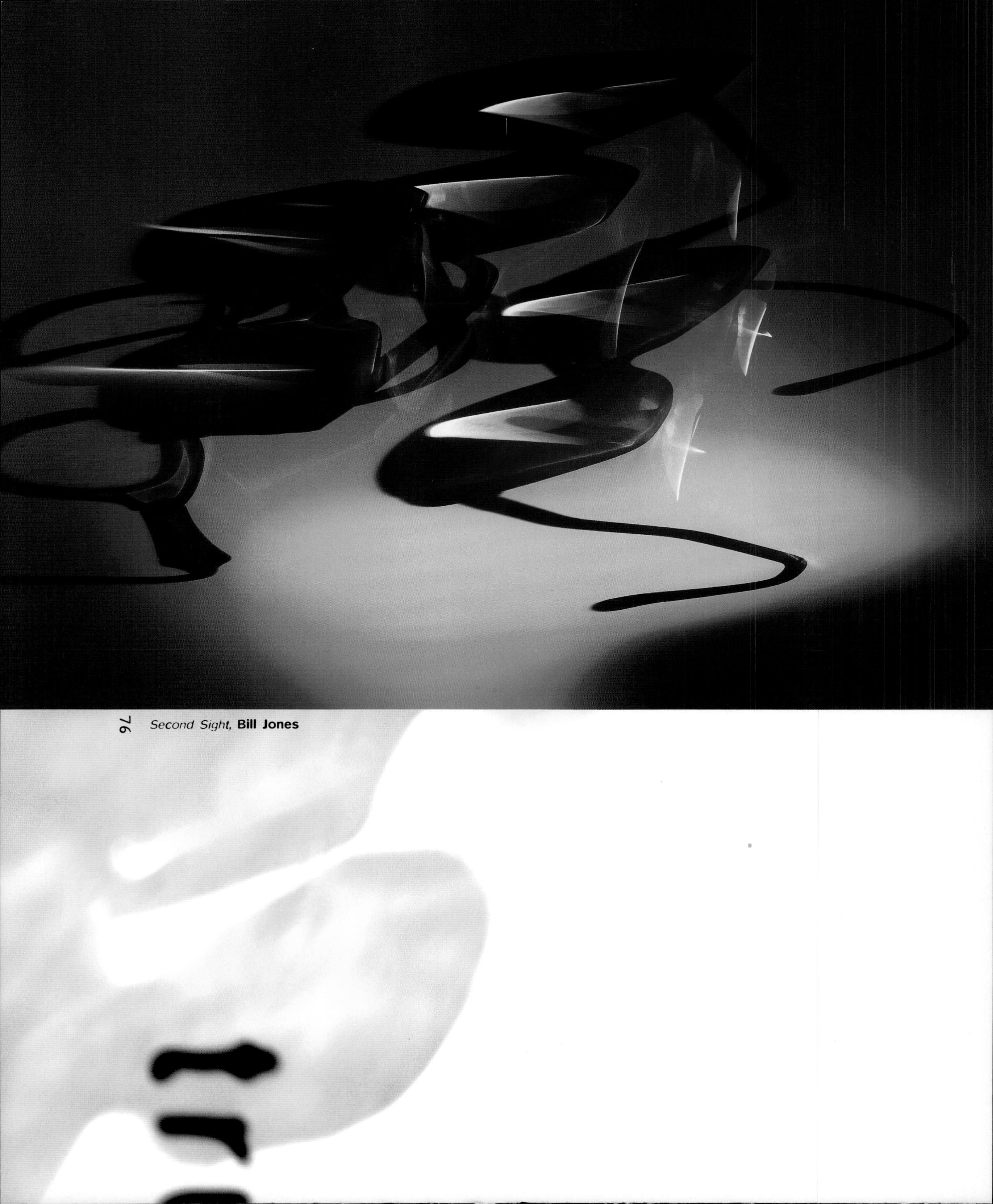

Second Sight, **Bill Jones**

Though *The X-Files* is the only show where my idol Ted Serios has actually been mentioned, my work is most influenced by the episode where Mulder notices that his family album is changing before his eyes. The pictures are alive! When the camera zooms in on the family snapshots, the people begin to move, but so slowly that you can't see it unless you look for a long time. When he tells Scully, she says, "Mulder, pictures are forever." And Mulder says, "That's what I mean, Scully, they live on forever." Then Scully says, "But you've looked at those pictures all your [illegible] Wouldn't you have noticed?" And Mulder says, "Maybe I've changed, Scully. Maybe I've changed too." At least I think that's how it goes. Or maybe I just imagined that all the pictures were changing.

Art-making is a process of organizing and reorganizing the myriad perceptions we are flooded with in our conscious and unconscious lives. In much the same way as religion or philosophy intends to make sense out of the world, creation of visual images serves a similar purpose. It is my attempt to articulate and record a point or place where the complex and contradictory information one receives reveals itself in a larger way. The finished work may not be a place to find rest in a purely aesthetic experience of beauty, but rather is a trigger which trips a series of questions and propels us through a less linear stream of associations. It may be uncomfortable, because it is not familiar, yet it may cause one to pause and contemplate more complex relationships between the worlds of physical, spiritual, and psychic experience. A collage of images is like bits and scraps of memory, observation, feeling, and sensation reassembled to resonate in new ways. The work may evoke a sense of knowing, without presenting immediately recognizable objects. It provides a gateway to individual associations, exploration, and meanings.

Guardian, **Anne Marie Karlsen***

Eye, **Lisa Kereszi**

To create this image, I used a flashlight to illuminate the subject's eye, which also blinds it. In the other pictures from the shoot, he is looking out the window, up into the sky, and the ray can be assumed to be coming from some unidentified source flying above. Here he is investigating, peering down into something, maybe a petri dish or a jar containing something unspeakable. The beam emanates up from the object. The light is so bright that it is all that he can see.

My interest in *The X-Files* as a body of work concerns its inquiry into states of sensory phenomena which often become apparent during what are presumed to be psychic dislocations.

DECEIVE

INVEIGLE

OBFUSCATE

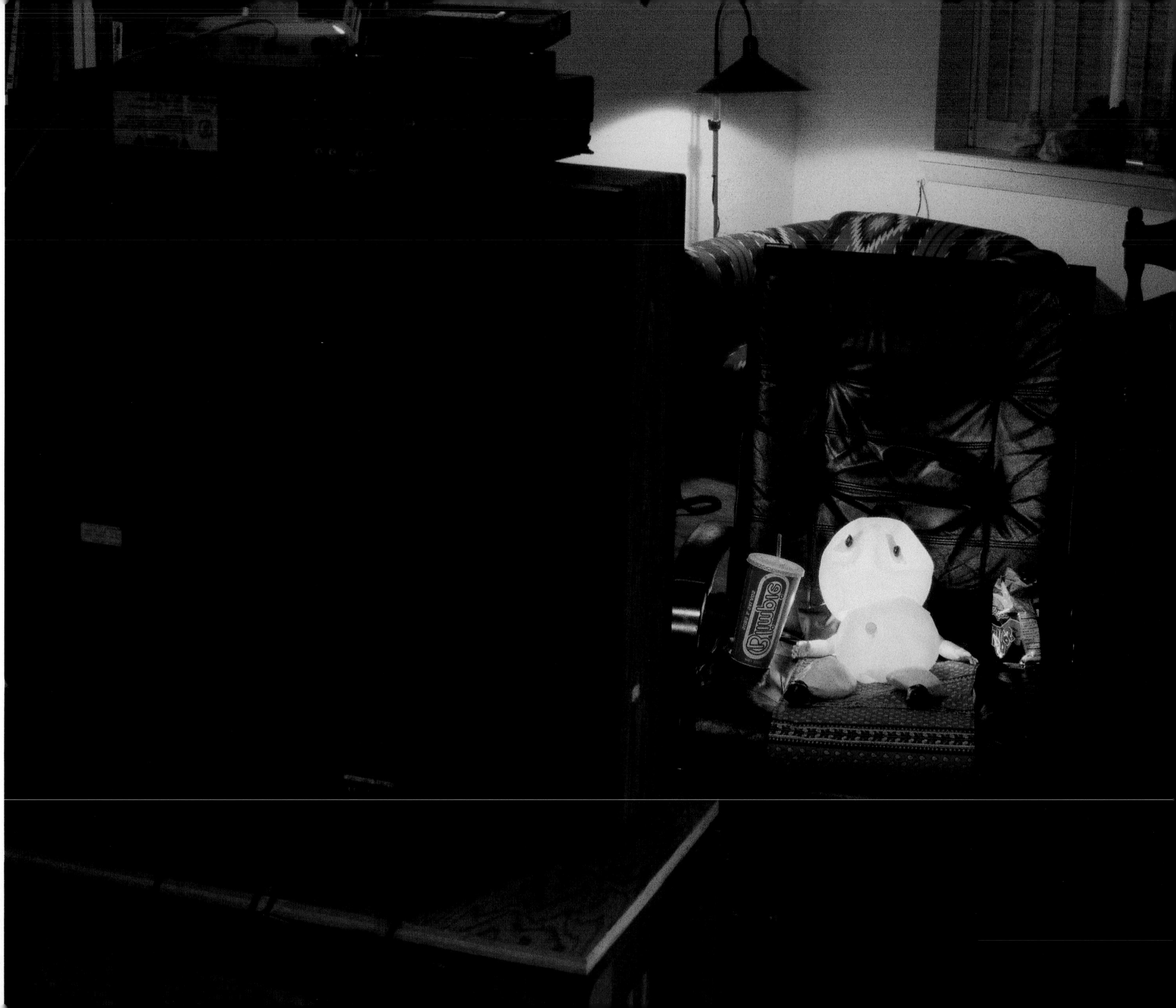

Watching **X-Files**, **Komar + Melamid**

Do you ever wonder why mainstream belief in 1997 is that aliens come from a superior intelligence and higher stratum than our own? Aliens have replaced angels in heaven and our faith in numbers and the scientific theater. In *Watching X-Files*, Komar & Melamid remind us that intelligence is relative and they elevate us from the couch potato to the couch alien, thus bringing us to the higher echelons of the gods. Here they bring us to the multitudes in heaven and depict our favorite pastime as the everlasting bliss it was and ever shall be. World without end. Amen.

Tell Us Something We Don't Know, **Barbara Kruger**

Our recent work is particularly connected to the issues and subjects that *The X-Files* examines, situations that appear to be of an everyday, mundane nature, but when scrutinized reveal possible phenomenology. We refer to an observation made by the artist Marcel Duchamp forty years ago.

"The creative act takes another aspect when the spectator experiences the phenomenon of transmutation; through the change from inert matter into a work of art, an actual transubstantiation has taken place, and the role of the spectator is to determine the weight of the work on the esthetic scale."

—Marcel Duchamp, "The Creative Act," a talk presented in Houston, Texas, April 1957

Untitled, **Paul Lamarre and Melissa Wolf**

Untitled, **Paul Lee**

I see Fox Mulder as a tragic
martyr of the system. He is a p
son completely driven by his
beliefs, despite being persecut
by the forces around him. He tr
suffers for his cause. I chose
depict Mulder as St. Sebastian

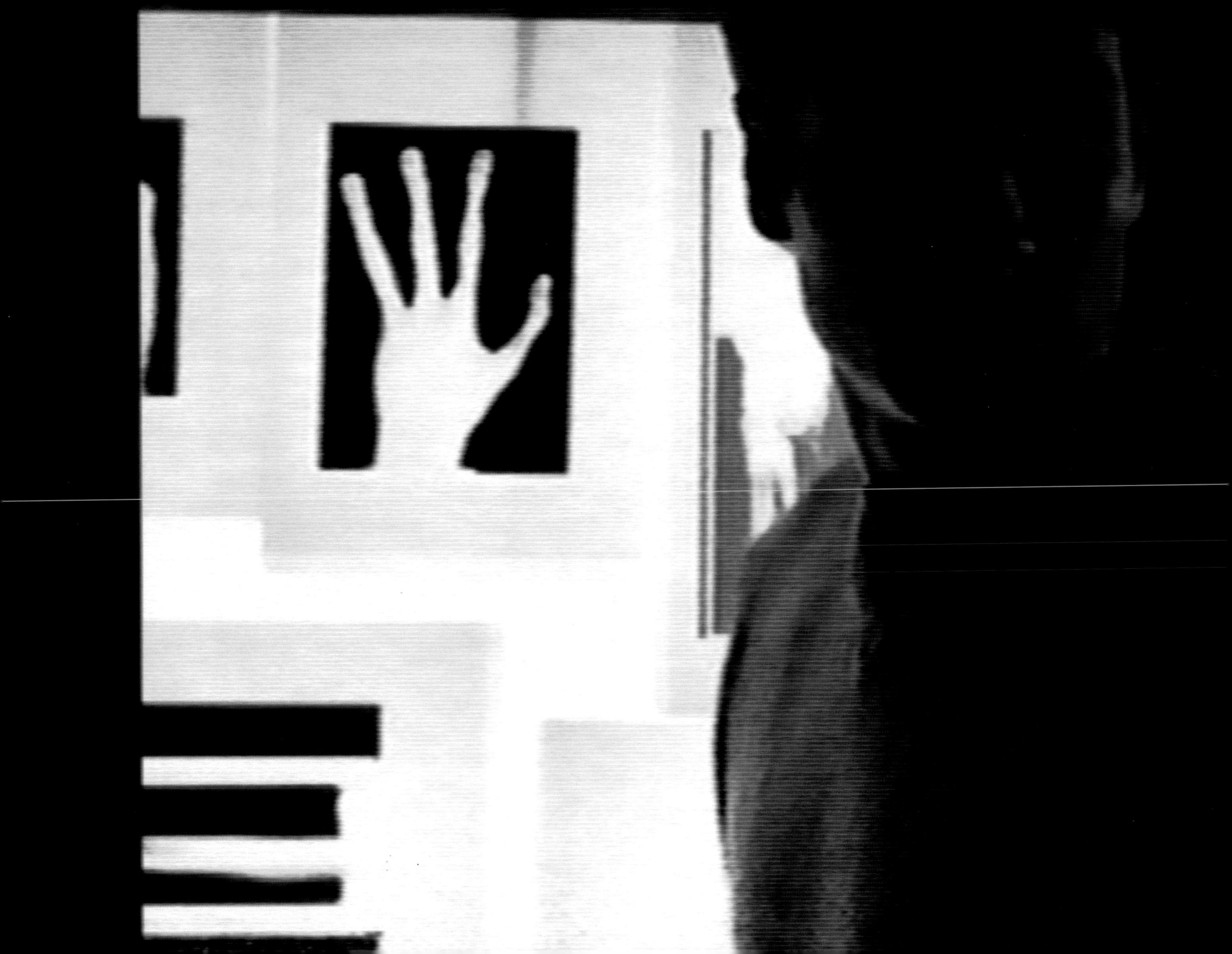

The X-Files is not your faithful, step-by-step, predictable whodunit. It grabs my attention. I like *The X-Files* precisely because of its loose ends and unanswerable dilemmas. I think we live in an age of too much information and easy answers from every kind of expert. Our unsympathetic, materialistic lives have been overly spelled out without the possibility of chance operations or imaginative interventions. Happily, *The X-Files* allows the mass audience (including me), habitually held down by numerous institutions like the dreary news reports, to experience the luxury of a questioning imagination. Amazing phenomena like astrology (conversing with the gods), past lives (history), magic, paranormal ruminations, and other fanciful notions that were traditionally the provenance of the aristocracy, are benignly incorporated into *The X-Files*.

After twenty years in photography, my work turned toward collaging cartoons and comics. As I learned to appreciate the popular portrayal of the heroic and the fear of the abject outside official churchly dogma, I could begin to locate myself in our time.

 Mask Death, **Minnette Lehmann**

E PUR SI MUOVE

Terminus: The Convergence of Matter & Anti-Matter, **Rudy Lemcke**

ehold I am ALIVE
For evermore"
Rev 1:18

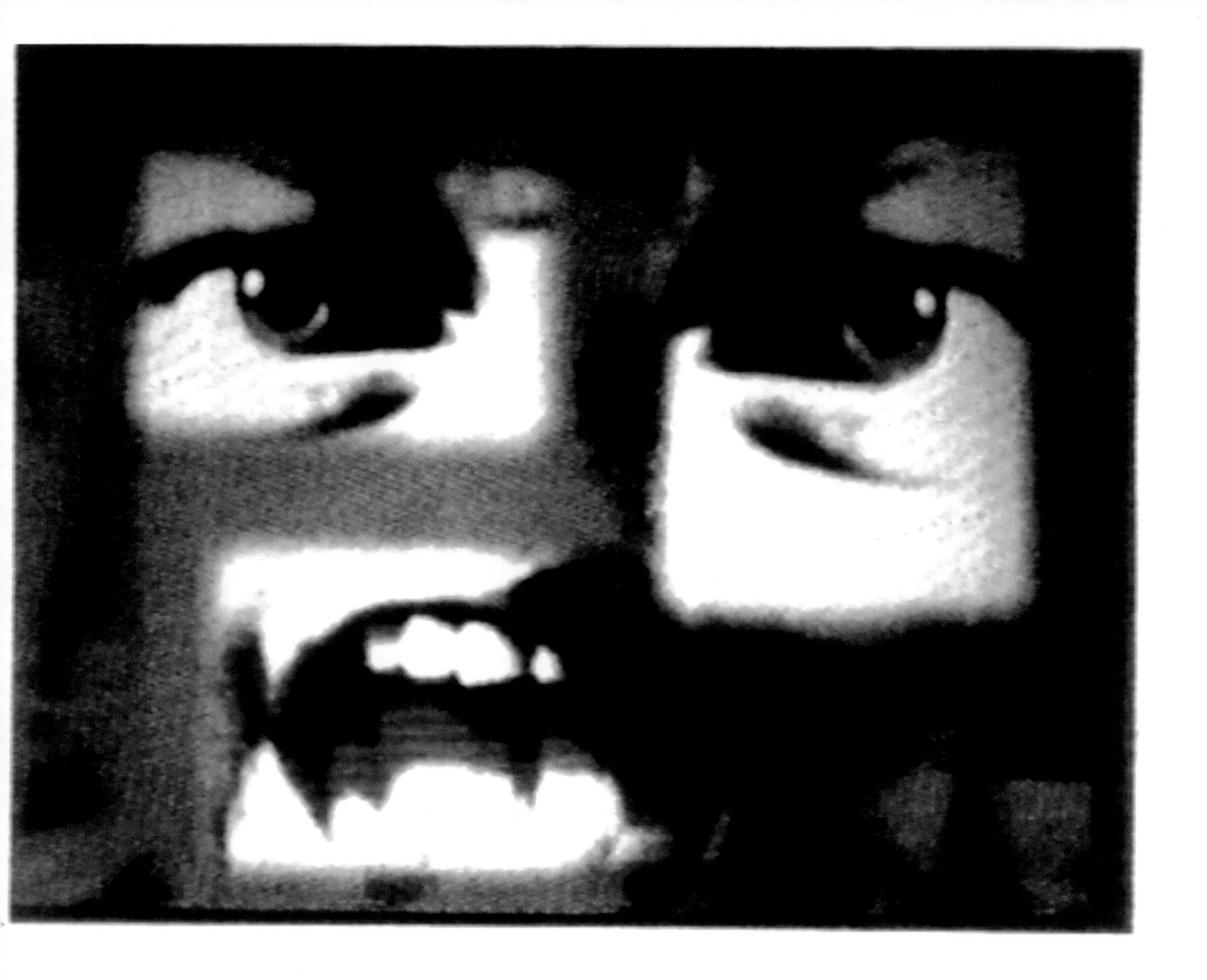

unmarked helicopter, **Vera Lutter**

The X-Files subversively contradicts our emotional understanding with facts. Whatever we seem to understand is denied, never confirmed. Doubt remains an exclusive residue.

The conflict equals the abstract juxtaposition of cognitive, positivistic recognition versus an instinctive trust in our senses. This, in my understanding, is the series' motor of emotional production; thus we can never feel safe.

My image shows Scully in an unconscious state, on a journey between life and death. We are unable to locate her mind. I seek to find an imaginative description of her condition.

In addition to the weird tales, I am inspired by *The X-Files'* dramatic lighting. There is the hard-edged, angled light of flashlights and headlights, the blinding light of ascending and descending UFOs, noirish raked light filtering through shutters and blinds. Light spills through doorways. Faces and figures are backlit, silhouetted, and illuminated by computer screens, electrical current, lightning. I am also fascinated by the show's rich complement of shadow and its generous expanses of deep, dark space.

Untitled, **Frank Majore**

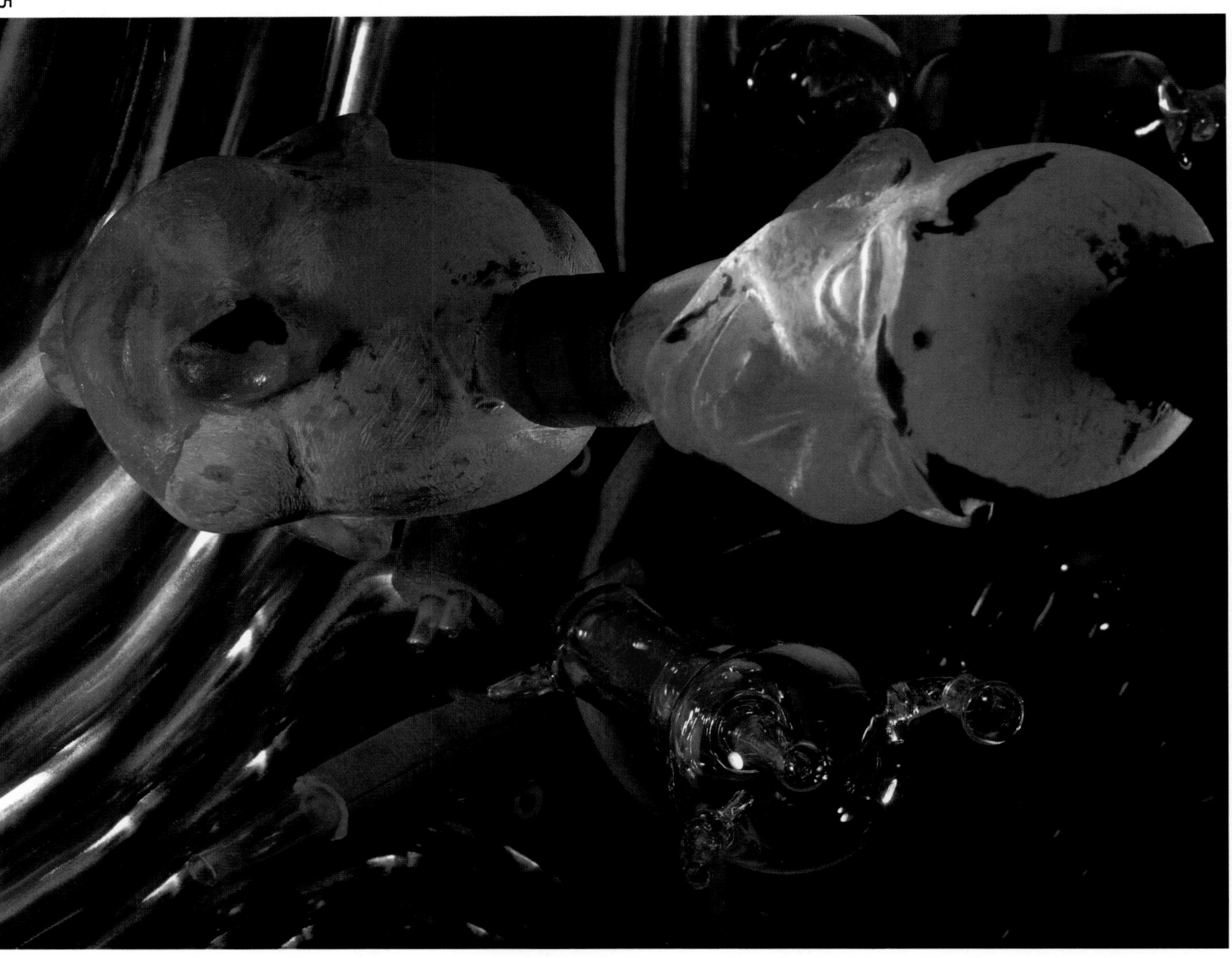

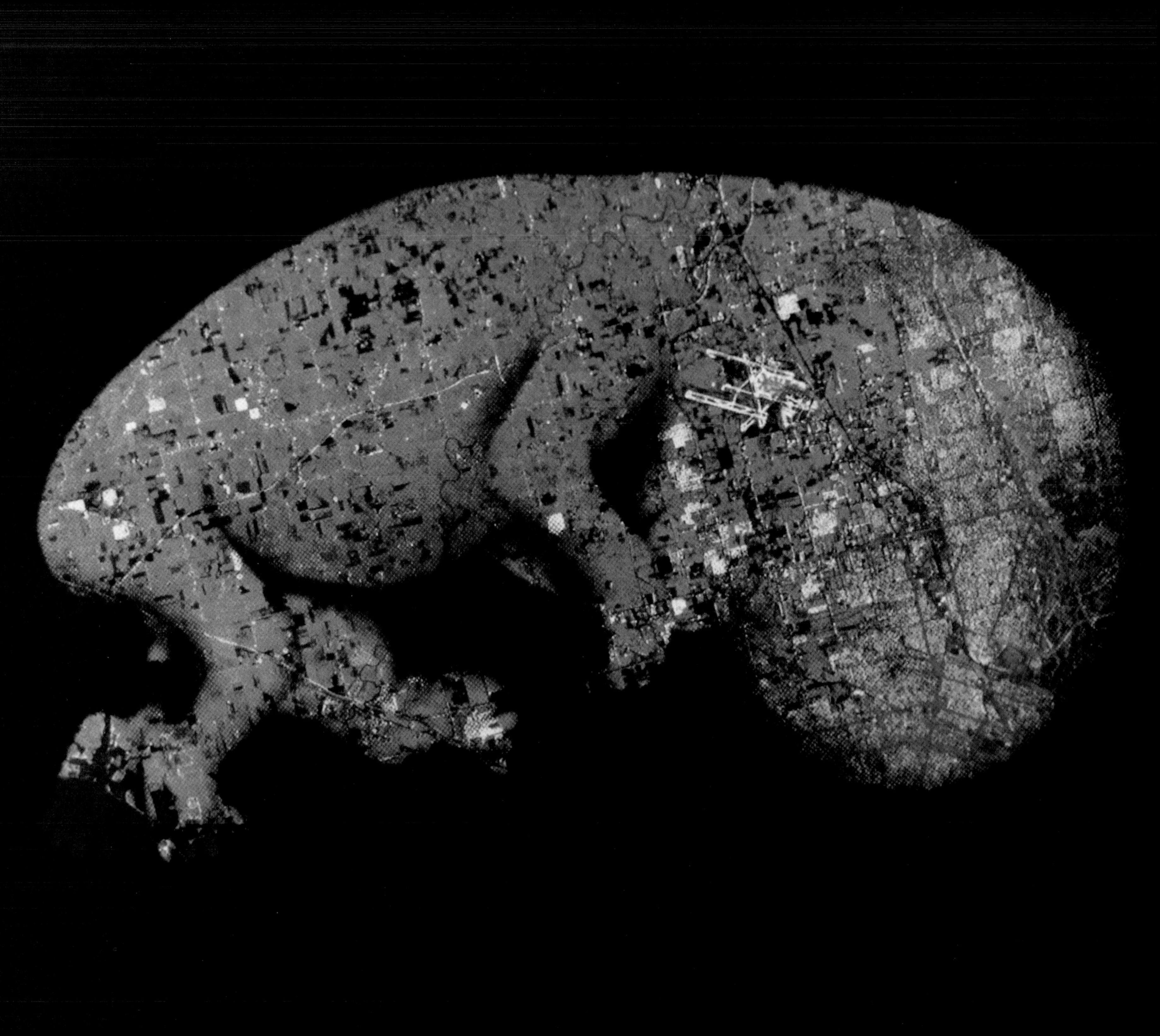

Synthesia, Aline Mare

The X-Files raises the
question mark of certainty
in the face of uncertainty.
My work similarly excavates
impossible truths in a
topography of the
unknown, where there
are no laws of the
imagination.

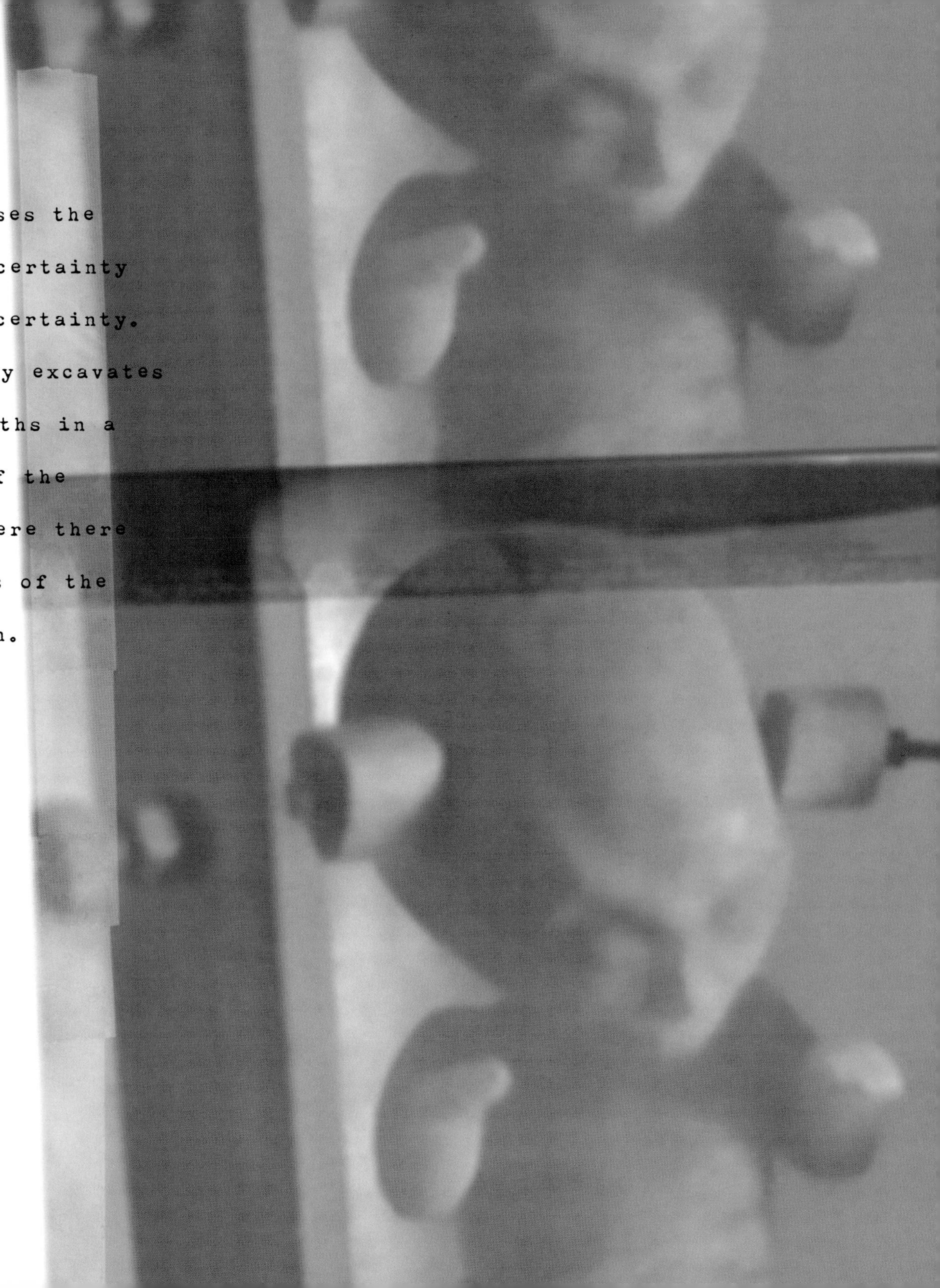

BELIEVE THE LIE

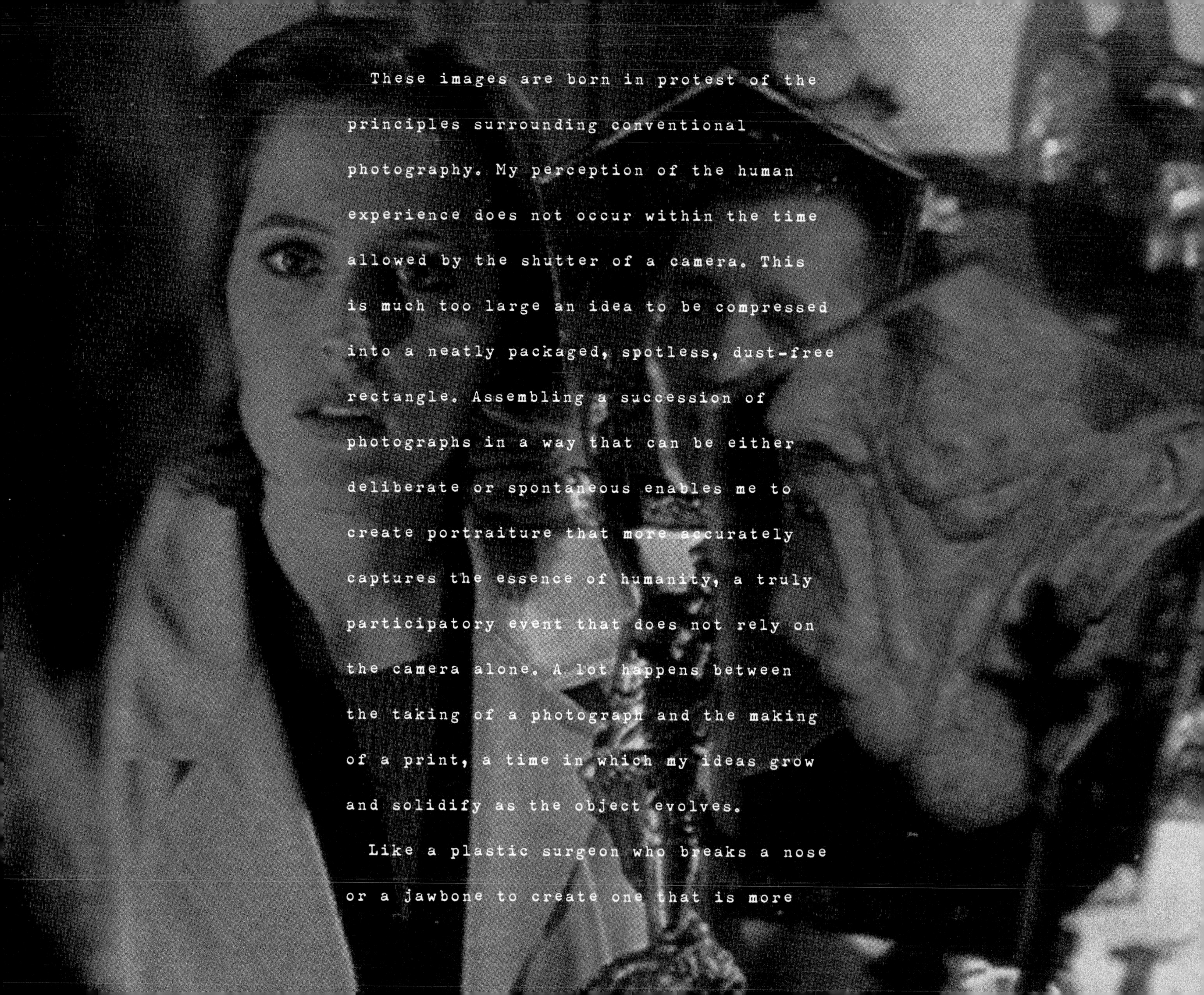

These images are born in protest of the principles surrounding conventional photography. My perception of the human experience does not occur within the time allowed by the shutter of a camera. This is much too large an idea to be compressed into a neatly packaged, spotless, dust-free rectangle. Assembling a succession of photographs in a way that can be either deliberate or spontaneous enables me to create portraiture that more accurately captures the essence of humanity, a truly participatory event that does not rely on the camera alone. A lot happens between the taking of a photograph and the making of a print, a time in which my ideas grow and solidify as the object evolves.

Like a plastic surgeon who breaks a nose or a jawbone to create one that is more

ealistic, I deconstruct an individ-
l piece by piece and reassemble
em so that the true human emotional
mental state can explode. This is
exploration, an exposé of the
eper recesses of the psyche. My
rk creates a complex, troubled, and
arred vision. The foundation of my
rk is to re-create images so that
ey are an illustration of height-
ed emotional states—desire, lust,
ge. The duality of the human condi-
on thrives in my work, celebrated
d exposed, not trapped within a
ngle click of a shutter.

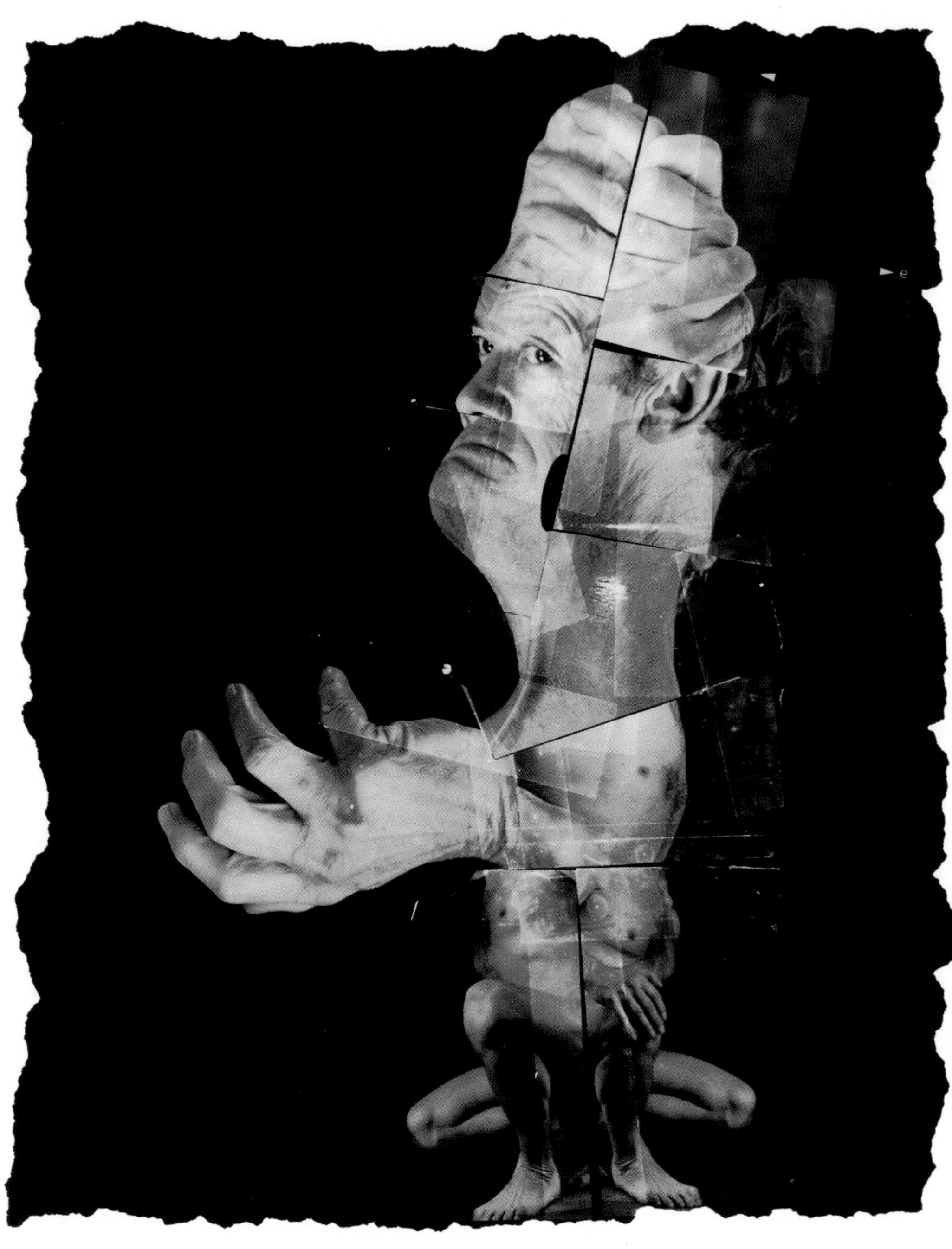

Untitled, **Clay Patrick McBride**

Primus Corpus

LICENSE SALE AGREEMENT

Genomic License No. 7 (Corpus Dualis)

For My Sister, Verna Marie Miller,
October 15 – November 30, 1942

BE IT KNOWN, for good consideration, and in payment of the sum of $__________ the receipt and sufficiency of which is acknowledged, the undersigned, Larry Miller (Seller) hereby sells and transfers to ______________________________ (Buyer), LIMITED LICENSE USE of the following described personal property:

**GENETIC CODE OF LARRY MILLER (PRIMUS CORPUS),
certified Original Human, born March 17, 1944, in Marshall, Missouri, USA.**

The Seller grants the Buyer license right to reproduce the Primus Corpus in its physical entirety as another human being (Corpus Dualis) with the following, exclusive alteration:

> the Corpus Dualis shall have only certain genetic code elements modified, and ONLY that limited set of genetic code elements at variance with the Primus Corpus, which together give rise to and effectively constitute a human being of the fully female sex.

Specific License:
License is granted for "one time use" only, that is to say, only ONE genetically engineered human being may be produced which utilizes the aforementioned properties from the Primus Corpus material. All remaining rights, including franchising, are retained by the Seller.

Specific Conditions:
The Seller provides the Buyer with the following body tissue samples from the Primus Corpus:

hair, fingernails, slice of tooth, blood

and the following body tissue samples from the biological mother of the Primus Corpus:

hair, toenails

The Corpus Dualis shall only be produced as a living human being if she is accorded the same legal and social rights as an Original Human.

The Corpus Dualis shall NOT be subject to any requirements by the Buyer and shall only interact with the Buyer on a freely volunteer basis.

Complete ownership and title to this specific issue of artwork and documentation known as "Genomic License No. 7 (Corpus Dualis)" shall be granted to the Corpus Dualis by the Buyer at the time of her graduation from high school, or the equivalent educational attainment, with no liens, encumbrances, liabilities and adverse claims of every nature and description whatsoever.

The Seller warrants to Buyer it has good and marketable title to said property, full authority to sell and transfer said property, and that said property is sold free of all liens, encumbrances, liabilities and adverse claims of every nature and description whatsoever. Seller further warrants to Buyer that it will fully defend, protect, indemnify and hold harmless the Buyer and its lawful successors and assigns from any adverse claim made thereto by all persons whomsoever.

Said property is otherwise sold in "as is" condition and where presently located.

Signed under seal this ______ day of ______________, 19___ .

Signed in the presence of:

______________________ ______________________
SELLER

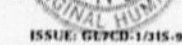

ISSUE: GL7CD-1/315-97

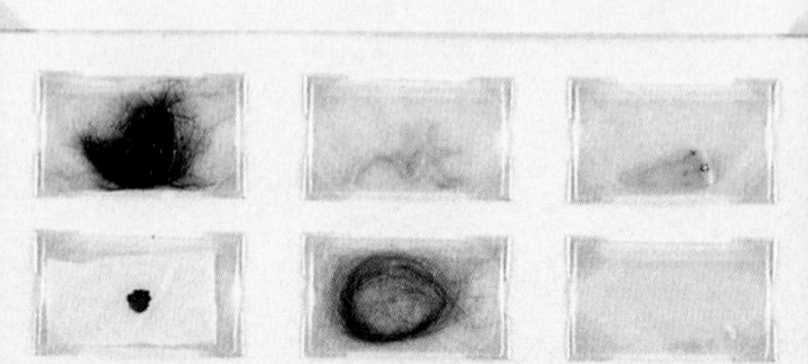

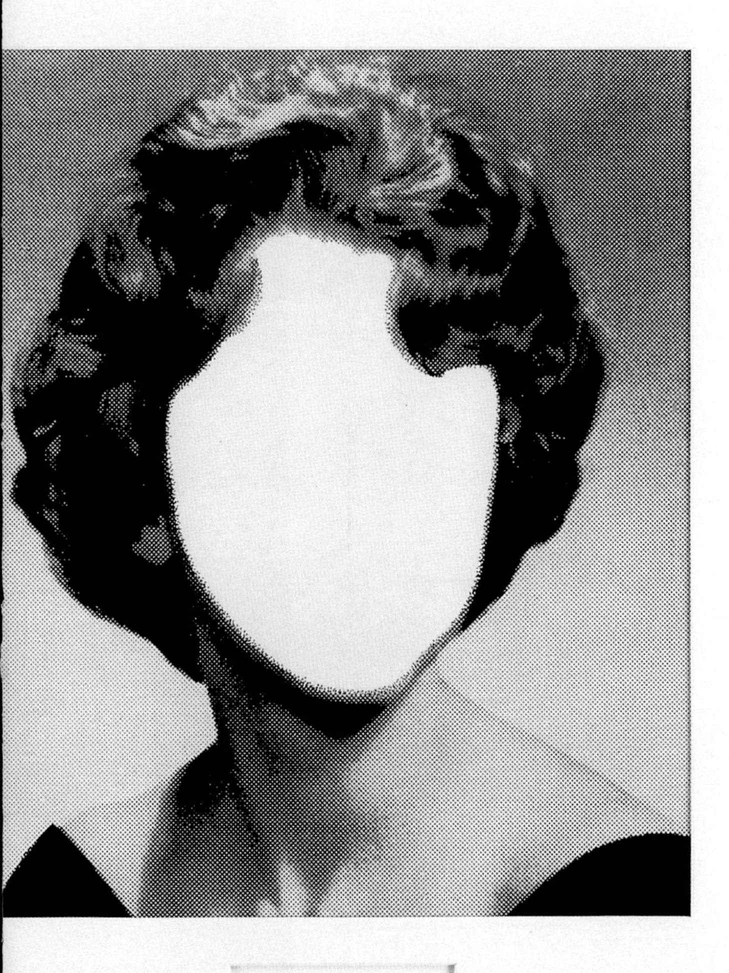

Corpus Dualis

Evolution is now a stock market option. The DNA molecule is the newest mother lode for scientists and patent entrepreneurs. But this powerful little object interests artists, too. A few years ago I introduced the *Genetic Code Copyright Certificate* as a grassroots way for Original Humans to claim some self-protections against the industry advance on patenting life forms. My recent work proposes that our DNA can become a material for the making of "art." With our genes on the commodities market in the neo-biological future, will inheritors of your code remain among the Original Humans or become part of a spectrum of engineered species from *Homo astralis* through *Homo zooid*?

The X-Files illuminates that art is a necessary companion of science and that Truth can be a Trickster. Like Mulder, I keep looking for a lost sister. *Corpus Dualis* is dedicated to her.

I suppose in one sense my collages convey the strange disjointedness and dread of people whose darker desires and secret deviances have overtaken the thin veneer of their socially acceptable personas. They are mindless impostors who are voraciously controlling and unwittingly controlled.

Untitled, **John Monteith**

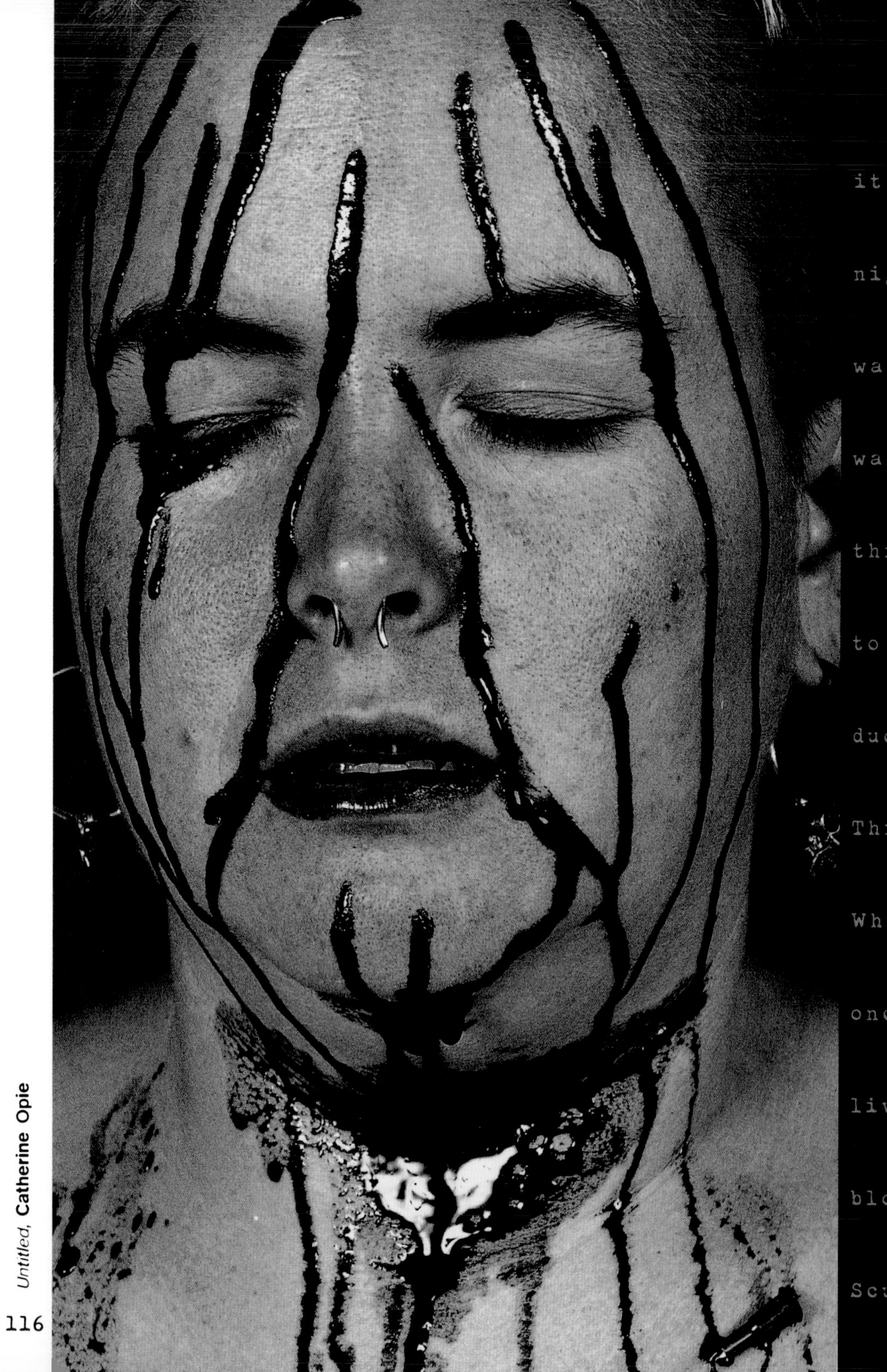

Untitled, **Catherine Opie**

The X-Files' Mulder and Scully are at it again. I have to wait for Sunday night every week. When I was a kid it was waiting for Tinkerbell to wave her wand toward the Magic Castle. Now some thirty years later I stare into the TV to unravel a mystery with the new dynamic duo—dry in the dynamic, but still a duo. This is what everyone wants to know: What is the cause? Is it the government once again being too involved in our lives? Why did she bleed streams of blood down her face? Who is in control? Scully, take a look at this.

My work examines the universal condition of blockage and impasse surrounding the temptation to lift off and accelerate. The X figures with arms up indicate the universal STOP symbol; they create a fence, a lattice, making a huge ring that surrounds a smaller ring of images possessing the universal symbol for GO, with arms down, at their sides.

This condition applies itself to the world of belief systems, which can also be impeded or set free. In this way, my work associates itself with an underlying message brought forth by *The X-Files* program, that of suspended belief. But it is a belief always surrounded by a larger field of pessimism or blockage.

NOTHING VANISHES
WITHOUT A TRACE

Let X Equal X, **Marc Pally**

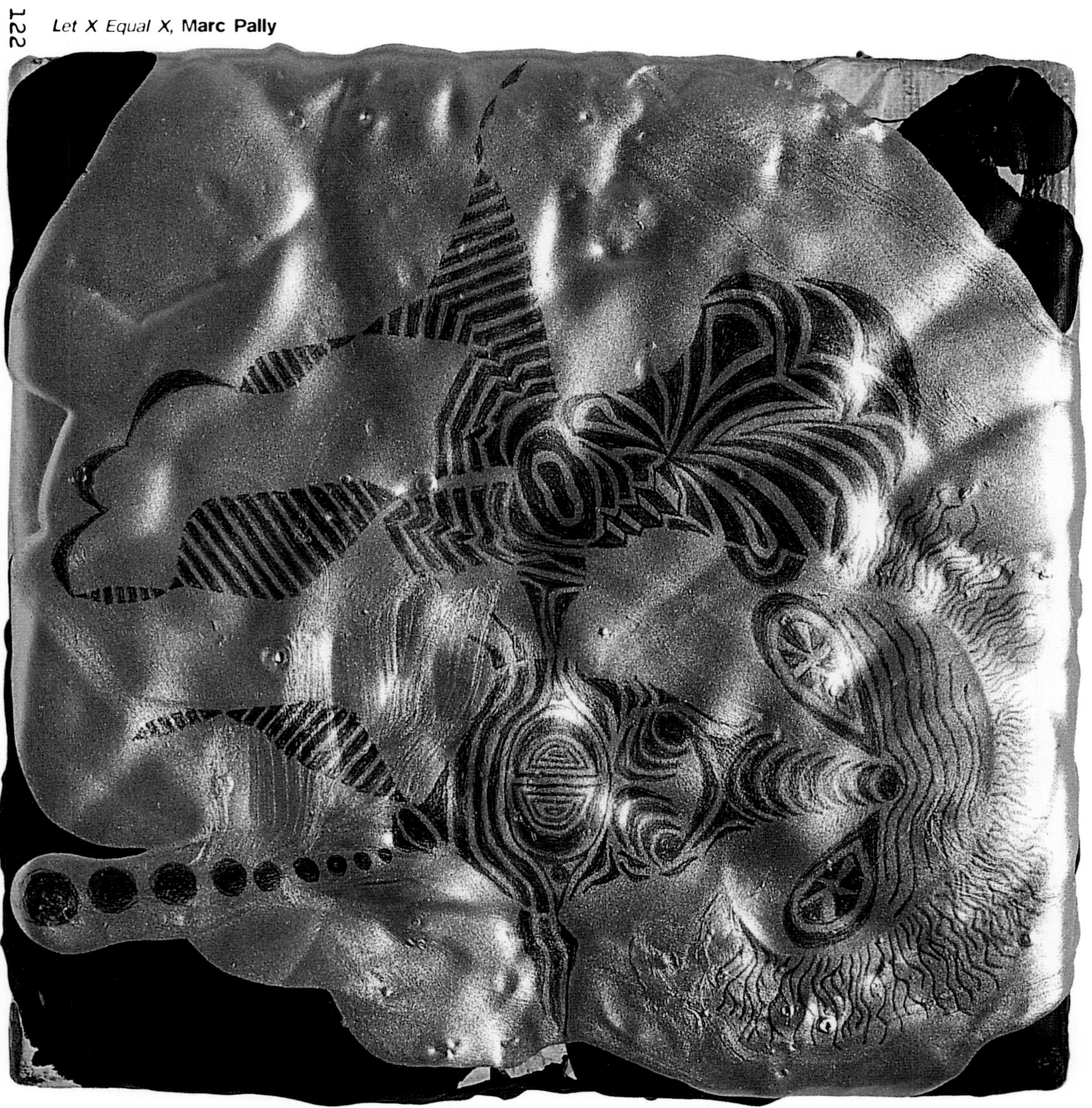

Let X Equal X is part of a body of work I have been producing for the past six years. The work is a drawing on top of painting, an inversion of the traditional use of drawing as foundation for painting. Just about everything seems topsy-turvy nowadays. Mostly the images are constructed and built up from small marks that collect and cohere into some sort of image (in this case, there is a specific figurative association to the image). I like the idea that the images are pencil—they can be erased, they are temporal. Likewise, the configuration of the marks appears subject to change—the rearrangement of molecules (or websites) is ongoing and instantaneous. I hope my work reflects and speaks to this state of constant transformation and flux, a place where boundaries are forever dissolving.

Light is supposed to be the photographer's friend, casting a shadow on photosensitive surfaces, bringing reality to a piece of paper.

But light can also be frightening—headlights coming at you on a dark highway, a stranger's flashlight darting through the woods, the glare of an interrogation room.

In *The X-Files*, light is fabulously threatening. Mulder remembers his sister disappearing into the light, while his own Polaroid camera flashes into Scully's eyes as she continues her autopsy of the next mysterious victim. "Please don't point that thing at me," she says to his camera.

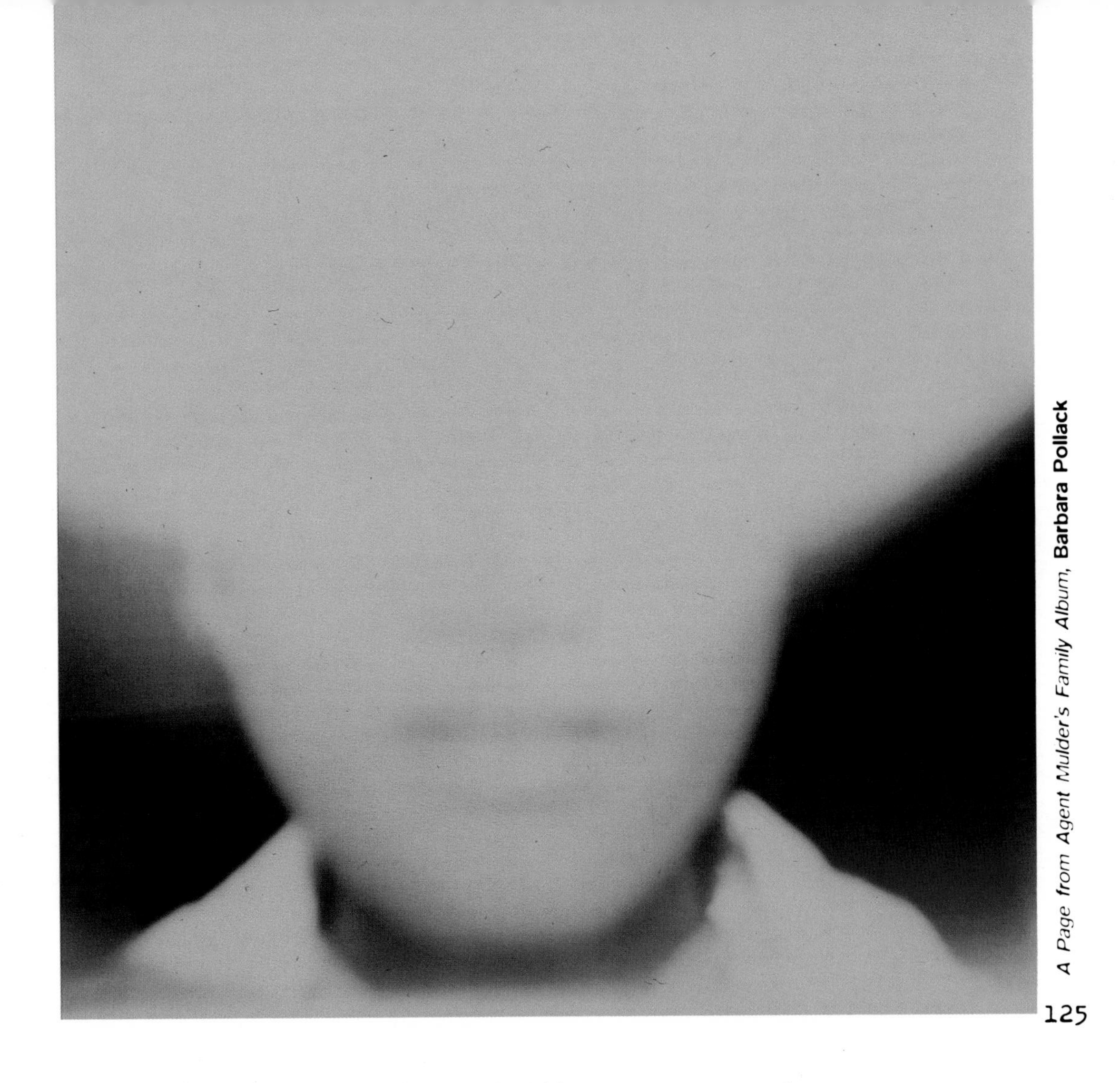

A Page from Agent Mulder's Family Album, **Barbara Pollack**

Max, my nine-year-old son, and I watch *The X-Files* every week, the way I watched *The Twilight Zone* when I was a kid. In choosing a picture for this project, my son immediately chose Katherine, saying, "Now, that's *The X-Files*. It's like the little sister being abducted by aliens." I agree. So, for this project, I've renamed it, *From Agent Mulder's Family Album*. And it is in Polaroid format, just like the camera Mulder often uses.

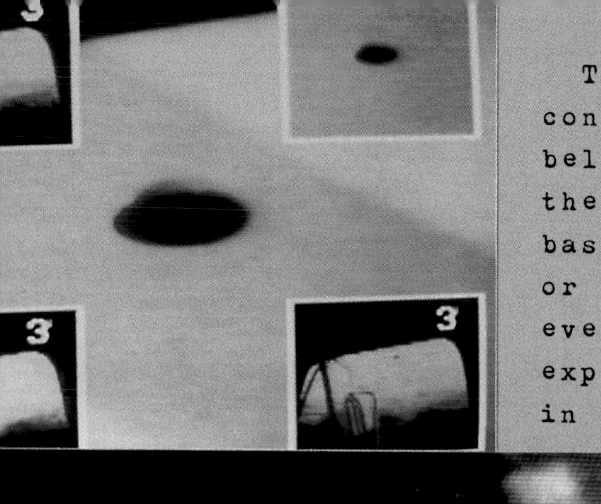

The worldwide reporting of UFO sightings, landings, and abductions is a contemporary phenomenon that challenges the effectiveness of our cultural belief systems on many levels, making it impossible to objectively analyze these occurrences in any one way. Mass visual phenomena has a historical basis rooted in religious occurrences, such as the sighting of the Virgin Mary or raining frogs and crosses. However, in our postindustrial culture these events (UFO sightings) breach the religious correlation in that they are experienced across a vast cultural menu, ranging from well-known intellectuals in the fields of psychology, physics, and the arts, to fanatical cultists.

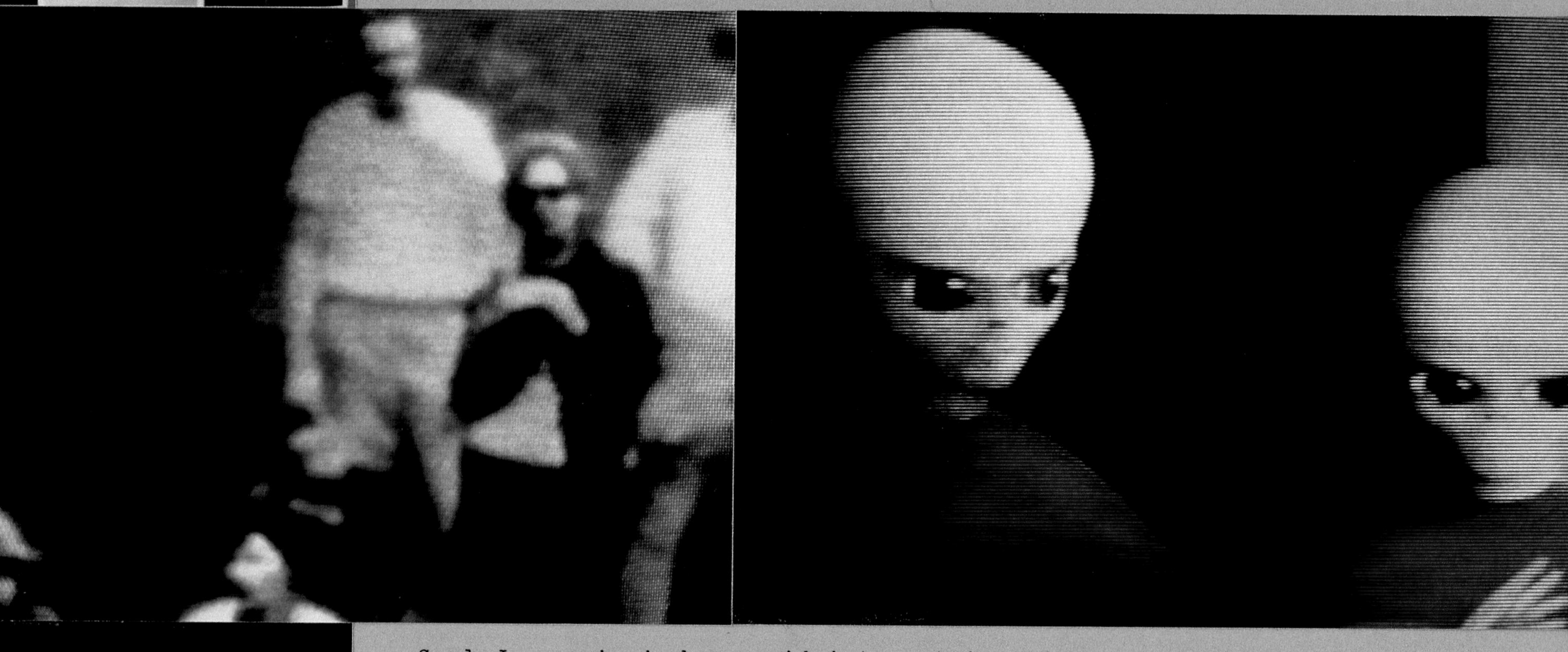

Carl Jung, who had an avid interest in this topic had no real answer himself. His exploration into dream analysis provides some insight into the phenomena in his concept of the collective unconscious. His idea of synchronicity, or meaningful coincidence, is another hypothesis that has some bearing that connects it with archetypal psychic processes. One that I find of interest, because I've seen this manifestation in the contemporary art world, is the association processes many people often experience of parallelism in time and space, with the result that different people can simultaneously produce the same new ideas.

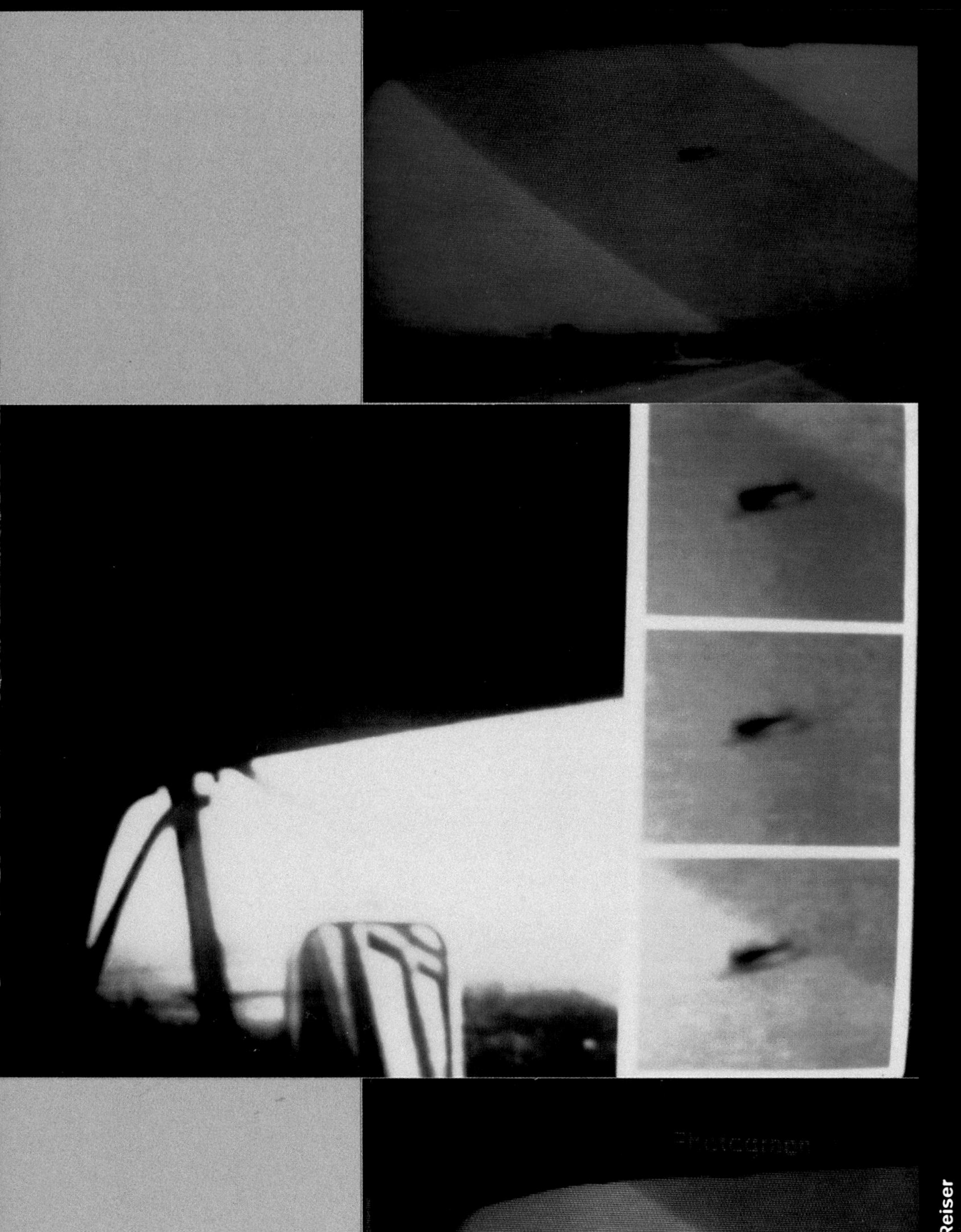

Untitled, **Daniel Reiser**

Jacques Vallee points out in his books that there must be 3,000 UFO encounters a month and this has been going on for well over fifty years. The political conspiracy theories are abundant. Sexual encounters with aliens are commonly recollected under hypnosis. Some of these I believe are real, others not. I believe that our cultures and religions have produced a state of psychic repression and rigidity that no longer provides the individual with their spiritual autonomy, resulting in the commonality of this global phenomenon.

Another concept that I concur with wholeheartedly is Terence McKenna's theory that UFOs are distorted reflections of the transcendental object at the end of time. His idea is that there is some kind of leakage into the syntactical continuum, and that UFOs are simple fluctuations in the syntactical machinery of reality and we're imprisoned in some kind of work of art.

Despite the synthesizing of my thinking approach on this topic, I deliberately refrain from assigning one explanation to it, allowing it to fall into the realm of the poetic rather than the didactic.

in the future everyone will be

abducted for fifteen minutes

Monotremes Unite!, **David C. Scher**

The plan dissolves in the daily observance of the ritu-

als of distraction. A calm pursuit of the fine thread,

fattening in a twist of perspective, cable thick in the

distance. Gravity, I embrace you.

DENY EVERYTHING

This surveillance shoot was done at 154 West 27th Street, New York, from 11 P.M. until 3 A.M. The camera used is a Sony 1/3" format CCD surveillance camera with a 6mm lens, recorded onto VHS, screen shot with EPY 160, and processed normally.

We all pretended to be *The X-Files* characters, some people naked, others clothed. My idea was to get everyone in the mood, and it became, well, a Hong Kong murder mystery/sex-charged psychological intrigue motif. White actors—Andrew Ross and Carol Irving—were killed off by Hong Kong gangsters—Celeste Olalquiage and Lord Der.

My work, over the last twelve years, has been about the incessant marking and tracking of indi-

viduals that takes place in our culture. I am drawn to the emotional dynamics of the cinemafication of everyday life that occu[rs] as we experience more and more of everyda[y] life as television and surveillance.

𝄞Reliability, availability, and performan[ce]

Television . . . reliability,

availability, & . . . performance!

Television explores perceptual control

at the beginning of the twenty-first cent[ury]

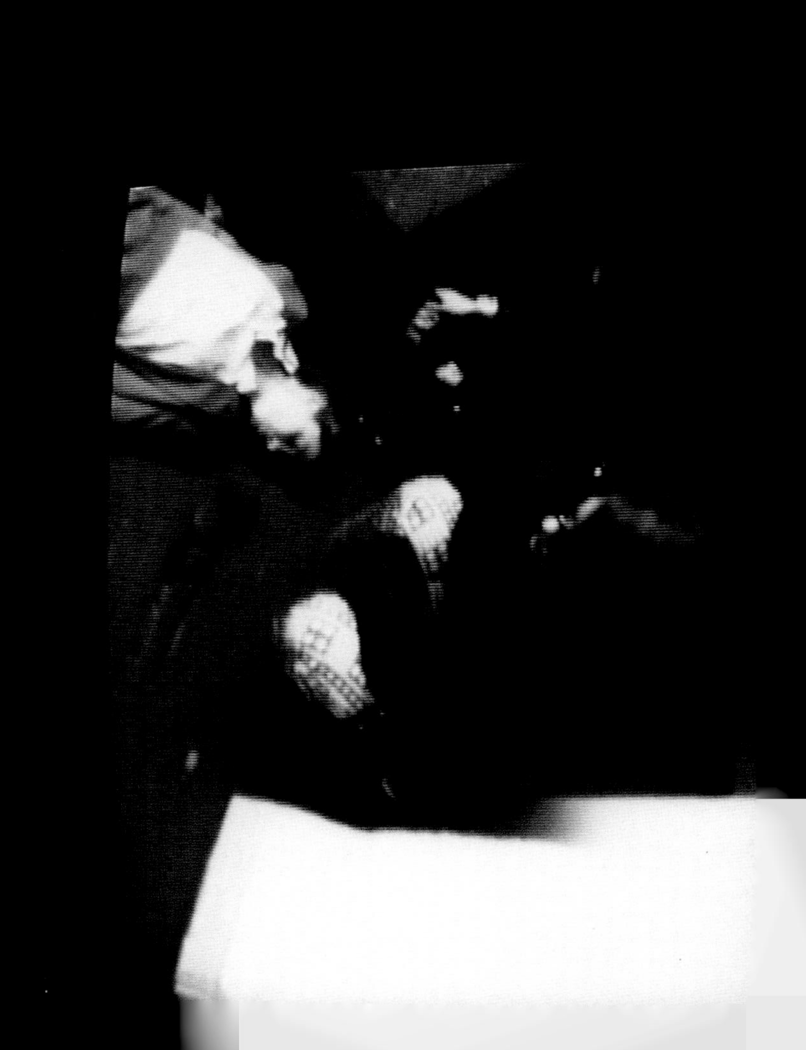

Untitled, **Julia Scher**

Untitled, **John Schlesinger**

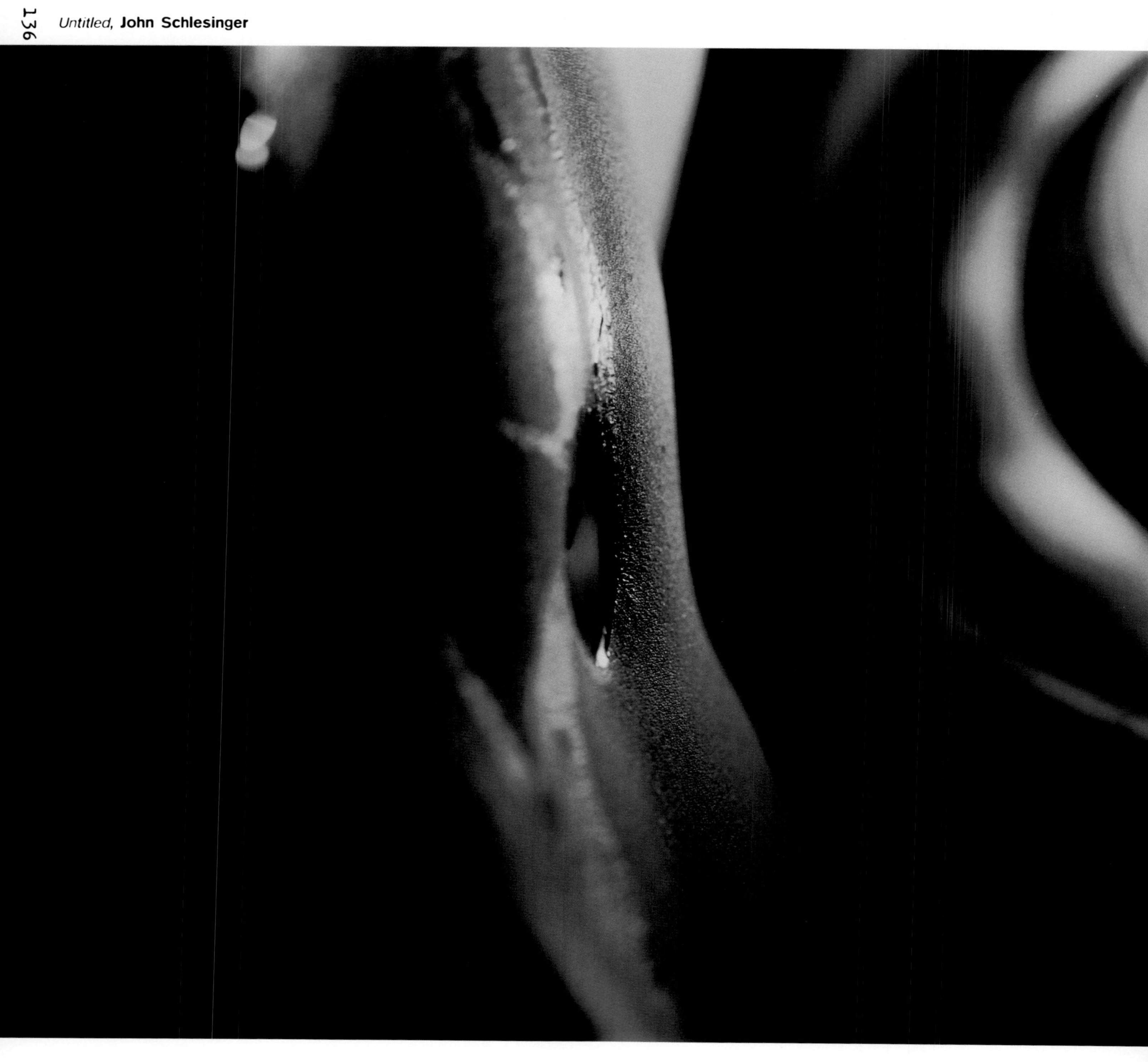

n Mulder refus
taste her bloo

"The Truth Is Out There" might be the mantra of *The X-Files*, but it is the lie that forms the trail upon which Scully and Mulder travail, deep into the corners that push through darkness to something else much more sinister and isolated. Each lie is a gift that entices the two further into the brush. Something is behind everything and we wait always, with bated breath, because something is always out there and in the end, the truth is anybody's to invent.

Soldiers Bathing, Schwabisch Gmund, **Collier Schorr**

Untitled, **Gerald Slota**

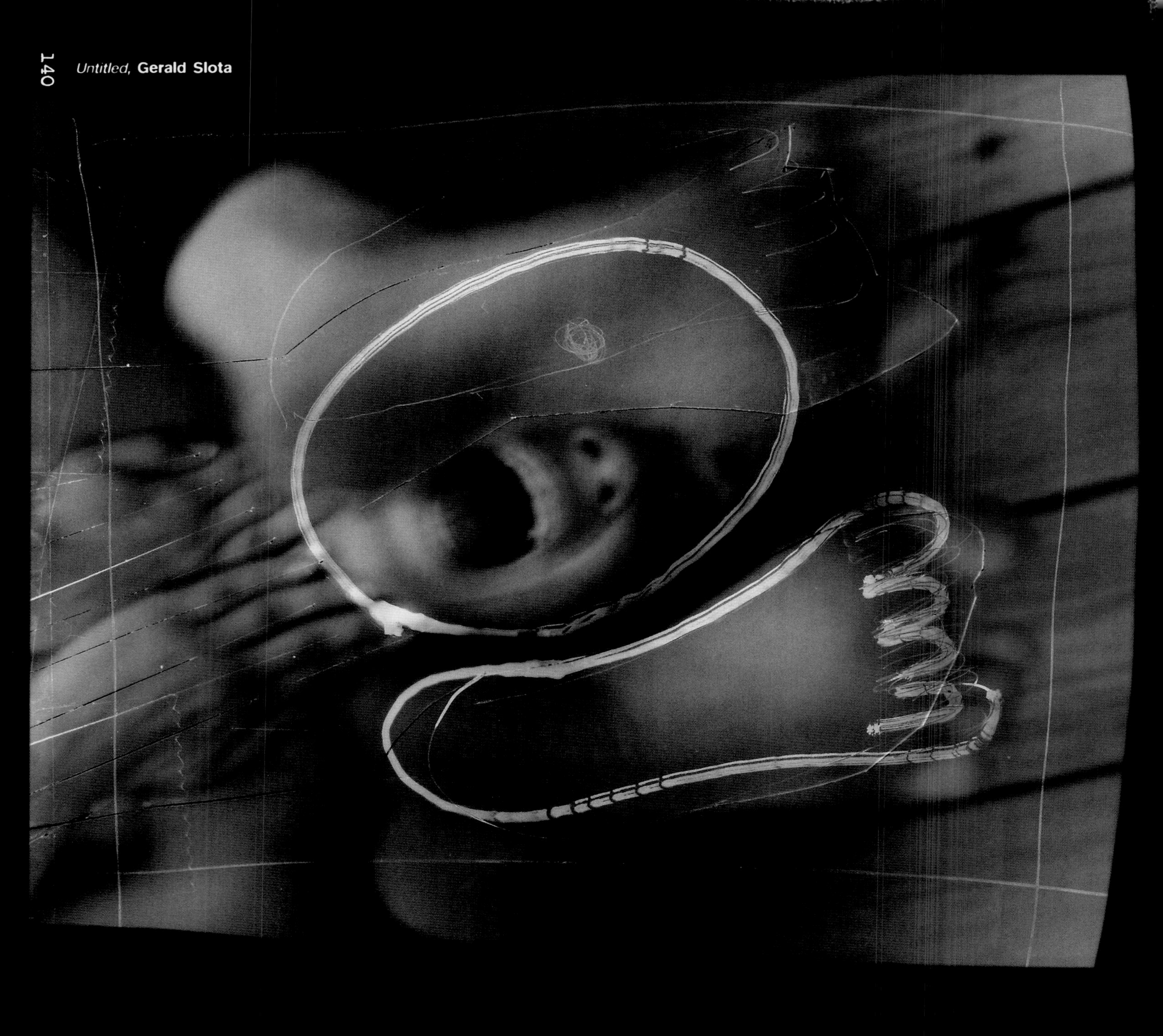

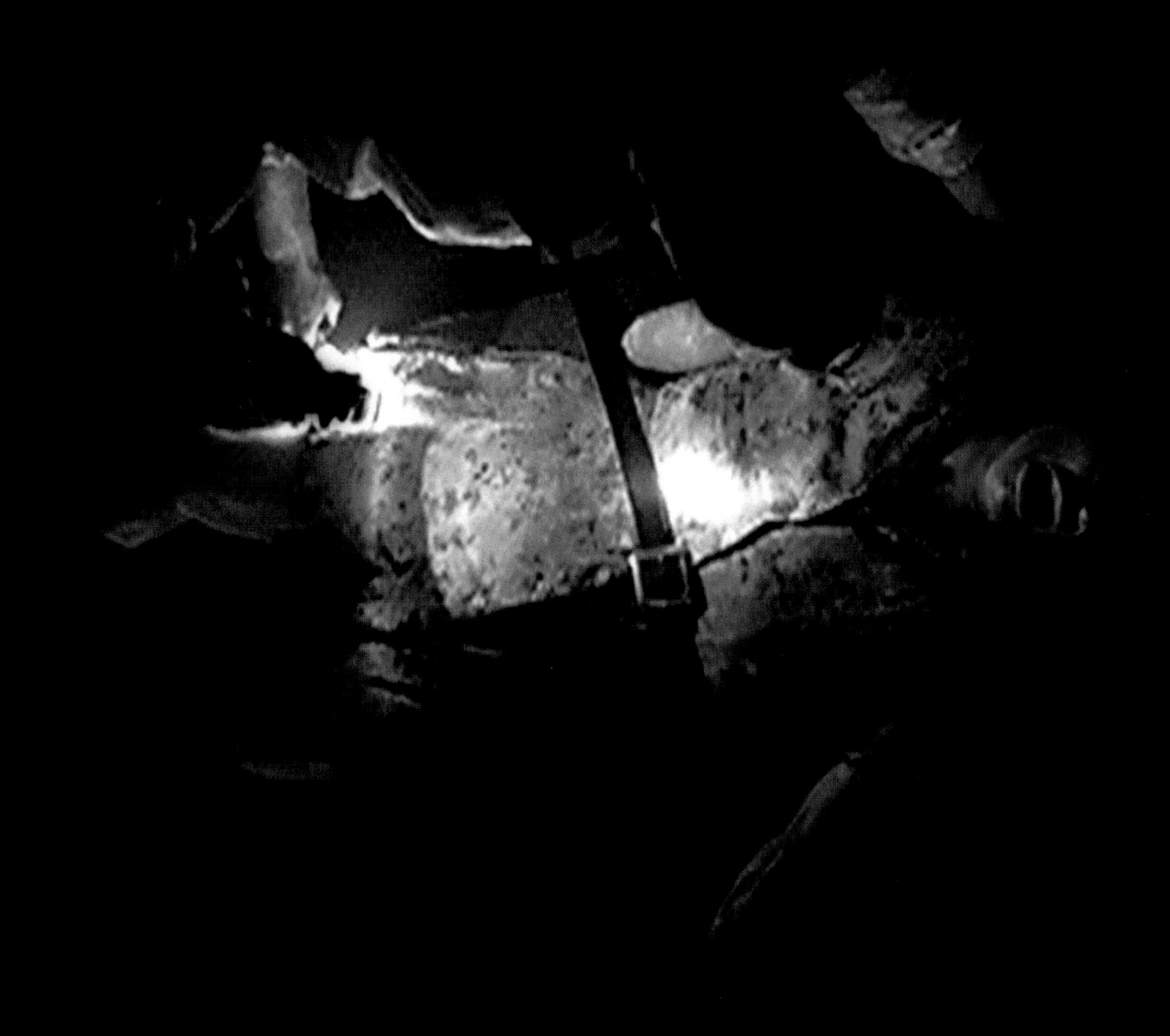

My work deals with breaking up the reality, time, and space within an image that has a different dimension, and presumed truth.

"The aspects of things that are most important for us are the hidden because of their simplicity and familiarity. The real foundations of his inquiry do not strike a man at all."

—Ludwig Wittgenstein

(The inability to notice something that is always in front of us is the focus of *Blindspot*.)

Mulder: "So, lunch?"

Scully: "Mulder, frogs just fell from the sky."

Mulder: "Maybe their parachutes didn't open."

Absurd as this exchange seems, it demonstrates the human exigency to explain and find meaning through allegorical or literal interpretation.

Other comments on this dilemma, such as, "Our big brains get us into trouble" (Vonnegut) and "The mind is a terrible thing" (Pryor) also refer to the pitfalls of abstract thought and a concrete world.

Whether our "visions" are only excessive temporal lobe activity or a glimpse into another dimension rests on the state of our continual one-foot-in and one-foot-out of this existence.

Blindspot, **Rose Stasuk**

ALL LIES LEAD TO THE TRUTH

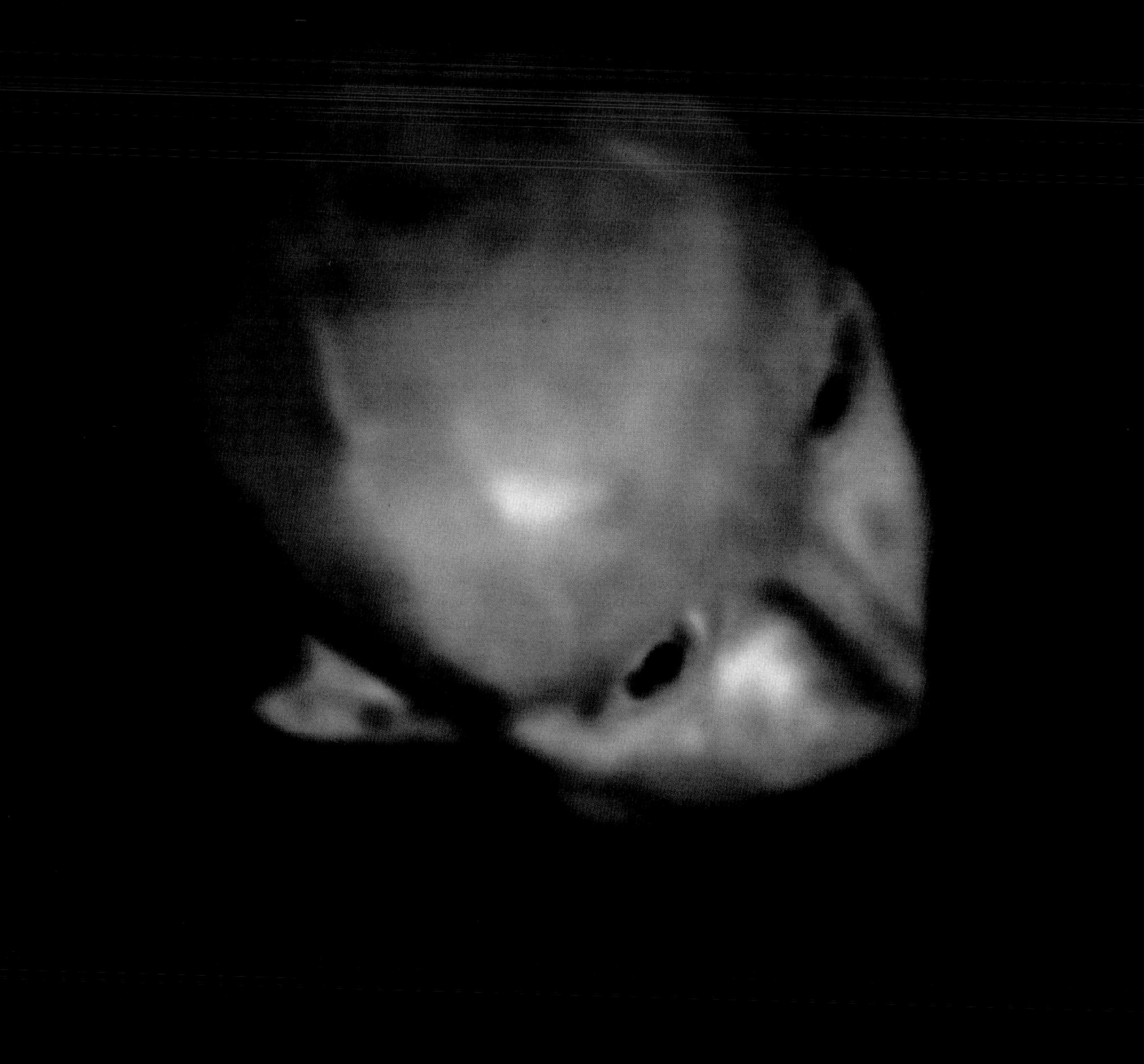

Untitled, **Robert Stivers**

I am interested in tension, in ambiguity. It is my hope that my images suggest a skewed vision of Classicism and Modernism, the spirit and the flesh, the profound and the mundane.

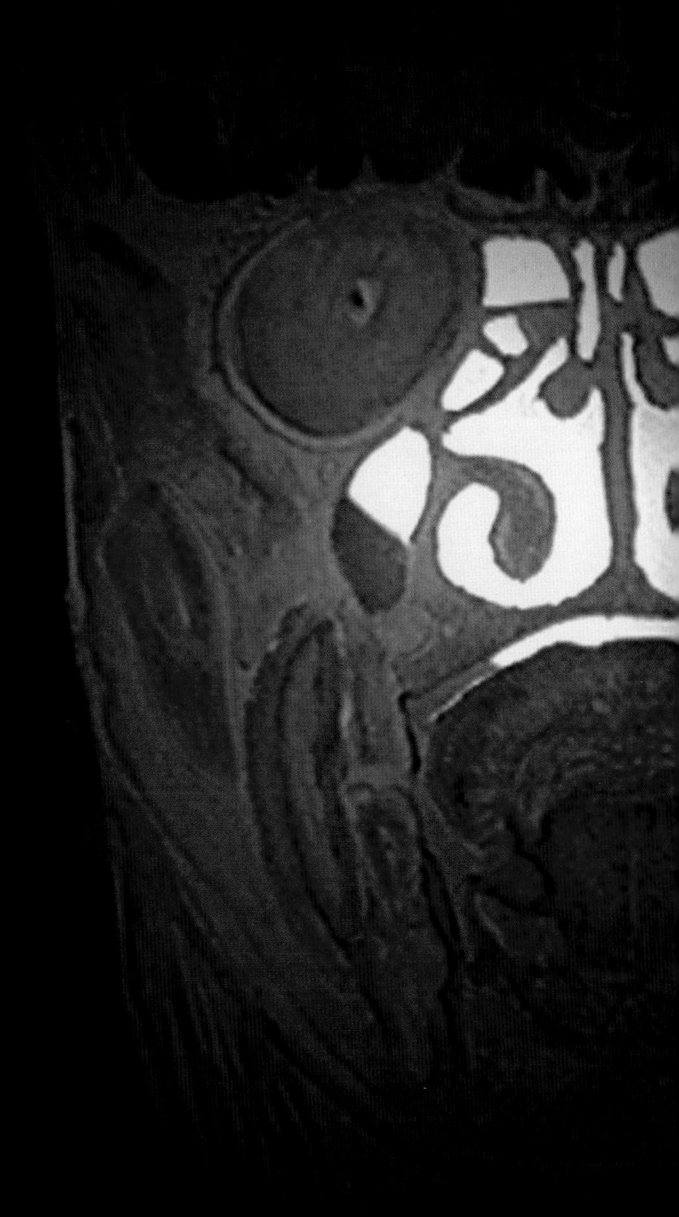

Untitled #313, **Oliver Wasow**

There's one *X-Files* episode I remember in particular. I think it's loosely based on the documentary *My Brother's Keeper*. It was about the three hardworking brothers who live in the farmhouse with their mother. The only problem is the brothers are inbred mutants and the mother is a disfigured torso kept alive under the bed. Not such a perfect world after all.

Darkness Into Light Turning Red & Green, Rosendale, NY, **Jill Waterman**

My photographs investigate events that are invisible to the human eye. Over time in front of a darkened scene, reality takes on unnatural characteristics as it is penetrated by light. These forces of darkness and light inspire my work and are key to my interest in *The X-Files*.

Excoriating Abdominal Emanation: Fear Actualized, **Ken Weaver**

I respond to the atmosphere and tone of the show, its sense of mystery, and its probing of various psychological states. I am also drawn to the displaced characters that inhabit it, to its use of black comedy.

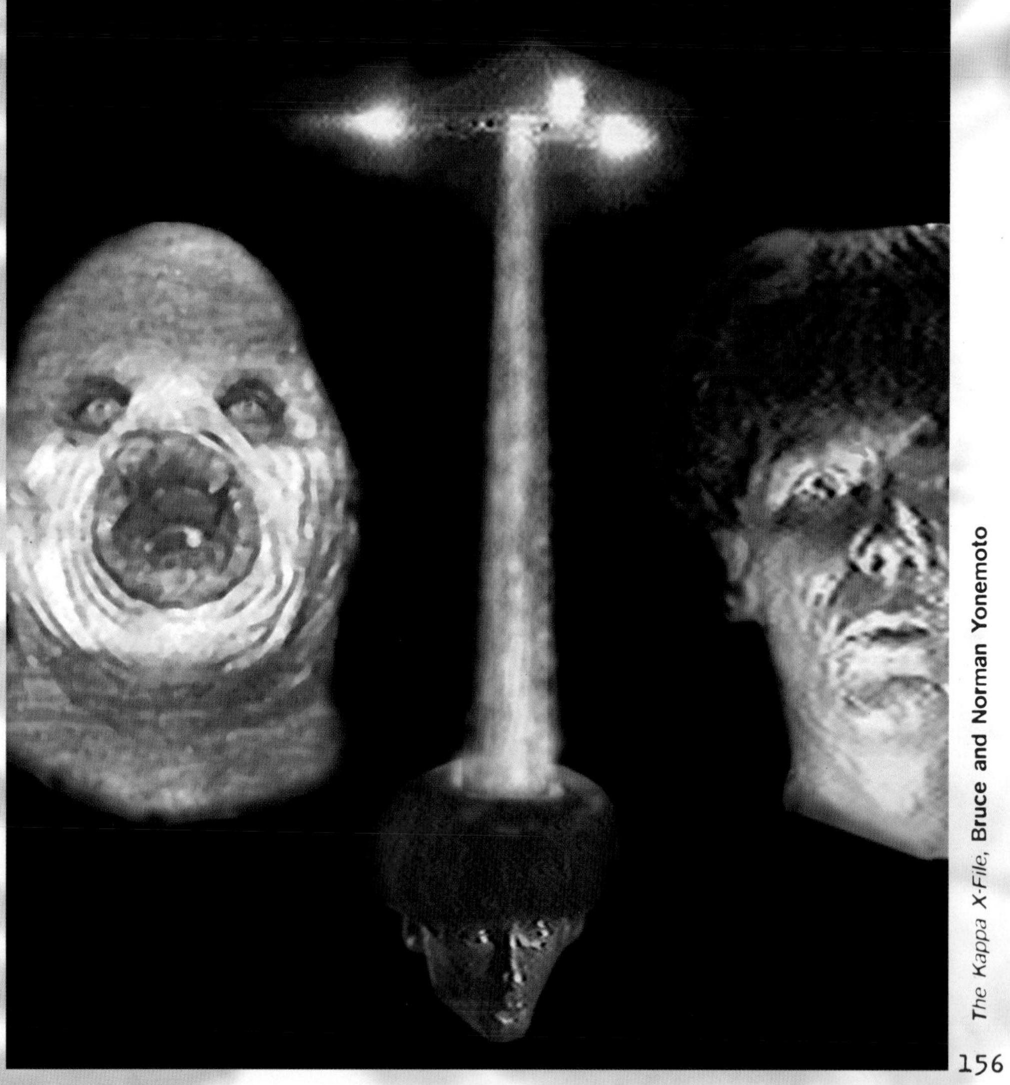

The Kappa X-File, **Bruce and Norman Yonemoto**

The "Kappa" (the Shinto god of fresh water in Japan) bumps into the "flukeman" of *The X-Files* episode, "The Host," in the sewers. Like the flukeman hiding in the Porta Potti, Kappa has been known to wait under outhouses along rivers to snag helpless victims. Is this a case of mistaken identity or are many of the creatures in *The X-Files* mutations of creatures in the myths and folklore of the world? And the Kappa has a saucer-like indentation on the top of his skull. A precursor of other saucer tales yet to come?

acknowledgments

The Art of the X-Files is a project that depended on the understanding, patience, and cooperation of countless people. We would like to thank each of the artists for taking the time to bring in "the truth" from "out there." Without their enthusiasm this book would not have been possible. Lookout and The M. Company & Friends also thank Mike Campbell at HarperCollins, Tanya Ross-Hughes and David Hughes at Hotfoot Studio, and Danne Almirall and Will Montoya Caperton for their invaluable contributions. We thank Kathy Brew for her indispensable work in securing the artists in the book, Erma Estwick for photographing many of the works, and Alanna Stang, who helped lay the groundwork for the project. Our gratitude to Kristin Barton for copyediting, and to Vance Lin for his contributions as intern. The project would not have become a reality were it not for the efforts of Pat Wyatt, Jennifer Sebree, and Michele Birkner at Twentieth Century Fox and Mary Astadourian at Ten Thirteen Productions.

CREDITS

PAGE 2:
episode: Kaddish
first aired: February 16, 1997
written by: Howard Gordon
editor: Michael S. Stern
directed by: Kim Manners

PAGE 7:
episode: Jose Chung's *From Outer Space*
first aired: April 12, 1996
written by: Darin Morgan
editor: Heather MacDougall
directed by: Rob Bowman

PAGES 9-10:
episode: Paper Clip
first aired: September 29, 1995
written by: Glen Morgan and James Wong
editor: Stephen Mark
directed by: David Nutter

PAGE 14:

Thom Ang, *The Expulsion from Paradise (The Original X-File)*, 1997; oil and acrylic digitally processed on paper; image size 11 x 10 1/4 inches; paper size 13 7/8 x 12 1/2 inches.
Thom Ang, an illustrator and designer, is known for his gritty take on icons of pop culture. Since graduating from Pasadena's Art Center College of Design in 1992, Ang has added to a growing catalog of paintings and designs for trading cards, book covers, CD covers, and video games. He was recently awarded a Gold Medal and a Bronze Medal by the Society of Illustrators of Los Angeles.

PAGE 15:
episode: Memento Mori
first aired: February 9, 1997
written by: Chris Carter, Vince Gilligan, John Shiban, and Frank Spotnitz
editor: Michael S. Stern
directed by: Rob Bowman

PAGES 16-17:

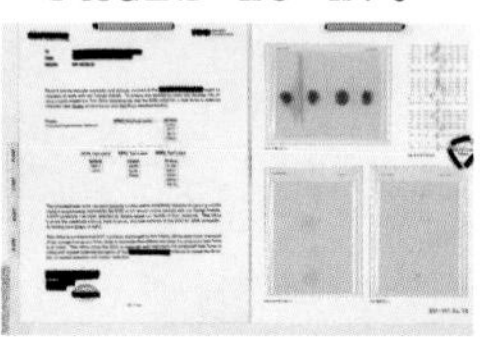

Richard Andre, *HTP-197.04.10*, 1997; ink on paper, blood, bone marrow, and skin on glass in archival evidence sleeves and file; 11 1/8 x 17 15/16 inches.
Richard Andre, born in St. Louis, Missouri, studied military law enforcement, investigations, and special operation tactics before receiving his B.F.A. from the San Francisco Art Institute in 1990. He exhibited at the 1996 X-Art Foundation in New York during the Blast Art Benefit and has published "ECM-1295: Circuit Board" in *Art Online*. He lives in New York.

PAGE 18:

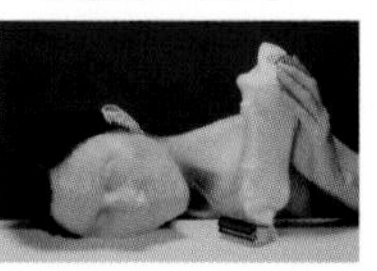

Aziz + Cucher, *Untitled (After Man Ray)*, 1996; digitized Cibachrome print; 14 x 17 inches.
Anthony Aziz, born in 1961 in Massachusetts, and Sammy Cucher, born in 1958 in Lima, Peru, each received his M.F.A. from the San Francisco Art Institute. They began collaborative work in 1990. They have shown *Unnatural Selection* in London and Milan and *Dystopia* in Paris, New York, and the Venice Biennale in 1995. They are recipients of the 1996 Ruttenberg Award from the Friends of Photography/Ansel Adams Center in San Francisco.

PAGE 19:
episode: Colony
first aired: February 10, 1995
written by: Chris Carter; story by David Duchovny and Chris Carter
editor: Stephen Mark
directed by: Nick Marck

PAGE 20:
episode: Redux II
first aired: November 9, 1997
written by: Chris Carter
editor: Lynne Willingham
directed by: Kim Manners

PAGE 21:

John Baldessari, *Goya Series: I Saw It*, 1997; photograph and text on paper; 17 x 14 inches.
Los Angeles-based John Baldessari is known worldwide for his innovative use of photographic images, his juxtaposition of found images, and his provocative combinations of images, words, and texts. Solo exhibitions of his work have been held at Centro de Arte Moderna in Lisbon, Serpentine Gallery in London, the Museum of Modern Art and the Whitney Museum of American Art in New York, the Museum of Contemporary Art in Los Angeles, the San Francisco Museum of Modern Art, Centro de Arte Reina Sofia in Madrid, and the Van Abbemuseum in Eindhoven, the Netherlands.

PAGE 22:

Mike Bidlo, *Virus*, 1997; color photograph; 9 1/8 x 7 11/16 inches.
Mike Bidlo, born in Chicago, lives and works in New York. He has had several solo exhibitions, including *Jack the Dripper at Peg's Place* at P.S. 1 Contemporary Art

Center in Long Island City, Queens, and held a performance piece, *Picasso's Women 1901-1971* at the Leo Castelli Gallery in New York. Bidlo has held a performance piece at the Metropolitan Museum of Art, and has participated in group exhibitions at the Los Angeles County Museum of Art, the Whitney Museum of American Art in New York, Frankfurter Kunstverein, and the Serpentine Gallery in London.

PAGES 22-23:

episode: The Erlenmeyer Flask
first aired: May 13, 1994
written by: Chris Carter
editor: Heather MacDougall
directed by: R. W. Goodwin

PAGES 24-25:

episode: Memento Mori
first aired: February 9, 1997
written by: Chris Carter, Vince Gilligan, John Shiban, and Frank Sponitz
editor: Michael S. Stern
directed by: Rob Bowman

PAGE 25:

Dike Blair, *Untitled*, 1997; gouache and pencil on paper; 24 x 18 inches.

Dike Blair, a New York artist, has shown internationally in solo and group exhibitions, including *L'hiver de l'amour* at the Museum of Modern Art, Paris; *Image World* at the Whitney Museum of American Art, New York; and *The Images of American Pop Culture Today III* at the La Foret Art Museum in Tokyo.

PAGE 26:

Gilles Chabannes, *Ezekiel: Tech Angel*, 1997; colored pencil on paper; 17 1/4 x 24 1/16 inches.

Gilles Chabannes was born in Paris in 1954 and emigrated to the United States when he was a teenager. He studied architecture at the University of Texas. Chabannes has lived since 1991 in New York City, where he works as an architect.

PAGE 27:

episode: Memento Mori
first aired: February 9, 1997
written by: Chris Carter, Vince Gilligan, John Shiban, and Frank Sponitz
editor: Michael S. Stern
directed by: Rob Bowman

PAGE 28:

episode: The Erlenmeyer Flask
first aired: May 13, 1994
written by: Chris Carter
editor: Heather MacDougall
directed by: R. W. Goodwin

PAGE 29:

Bruce Charlesworth, *Untitled*, 1997; Cibachrome print; 23 x 23 inches.

Bruce Charlesworth is an artist whose work embraces a wide range of media. His photographs, photo-novellas, tableaux, and complex multimedia environments have been shown in art museums and galleries throughout the United States and Europe. Charlesworth has written many screenplays and works of short fiction and has directed and designed over a dozen of his own projects for film, video, and theater. He is currently editing his first feature-length film, *Private Enemy-Public Eye*.

PAGE 30:

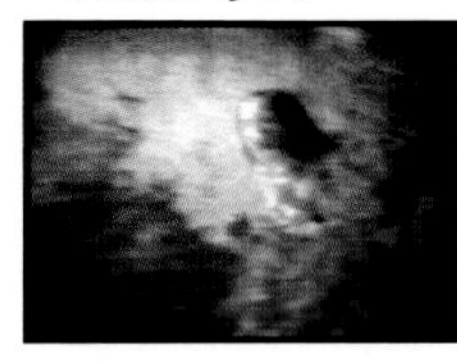

Karen Cinorre, *Still from "Toxic Shock,"* 1997; scanned photograph digitally manipulated; 5 x 7 inches.

Karen Cinorre is an award-winning filmmaker/video artist who works in the production, distribution, and promotion of media arts. She is the Executive Director of Drift Distribution and the founder of Ximira Pictures, both based in New York.

PAGE 31:

episode: Demons
first aired: May 11, 1997
written by: R. W. Goodwin
editor: Heather MacDougall
directed by: Kim Manners

PAGES 32-33:

Eugene Clark, *Postabduction: Mouth, Glove, Debris*, 1997; three video prints; image size 2 15/16 x 4 inches each, paper size 3 15/16 x 5 1/2 inches each.

Eugene Clark, a native of the midwest, studied at the Center for Creative Studies in Detroit and the Cranbrook Academy of Art in Bloomfield Hills, Michigan. His multimedia works incorporate photography, video, sound installation, and performance. He has staged one-person performances at the Detroit Institute of Arts, the Metropolitan Museum of Art in New York, and the Guggenheim Museum in Soho. He was a featured artist at the Fifth Soho Arts Festival. Clark currently lives in Brooklyn.

PAGE 33:

episode: Tempus Fugit
first aired: March 16, 1997
written by: Chris Carter and Frank Spotnitz
editor: Heather MacDougall
directed by: Rob Bowman

PAGE 34:

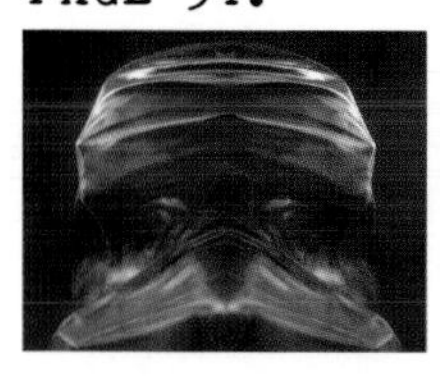

Barbara C. Crane, *Doppelganger*, 1996; digital print; 18 x 24 inches.

Barbara C. Crane received a B.F.A. from the Rhode Island School of Design, studied film history at Harvard University, and video documentary at the Global Village in New York. She works with a variety of media, including watercolor, collage, photography, and video. Among her video projects are *A History of American Art*, a video on the artist's plight in Soho, and a collaboration on the award-winning documentary *The Secrets of the Sphinx*.

PAGE 35:

episode: One Breath
first aired: November 11, 1994
written by: Glen Morgan and James Wong
editor: James Coblentz
directed by: R. W. Goodwin

PAGE 37:

episode: Musings of a Cigarette-Smoking Man
first aired: November 17, 1996
written by: Glen Morgan
editor: Jim Gross
directed by: James Wong

PAGE 38:

episode: Clyde Bruckman's Final Repose
first aired: October 13, 1995
written by: Darin Morgan
editor: Stephen Mark
directed by: David Nutter

PAGE 39:

Gregory Crewdson, *Untitled*, 1996; Ektacolor print; image size 7½ x 9 7/16 inches, paper size 7 15/16 x 10 inches.

Gregory Crewdson received his B.F.A. at State University of New York at Purchase, and his M.F.A. at Yale University. He has exhibited widely in the United States and Europe, and his work is represented in the Museum of Modern Art, the Whitney Museum of American Art, the Metropolitan Museum of Art, and the Los Angeles County Museum of Art. He is currently a professor at Yale University. Gregory Crewdson's work appears courtesy of Luhring Augustine Gallery.

PAGES 40–41:

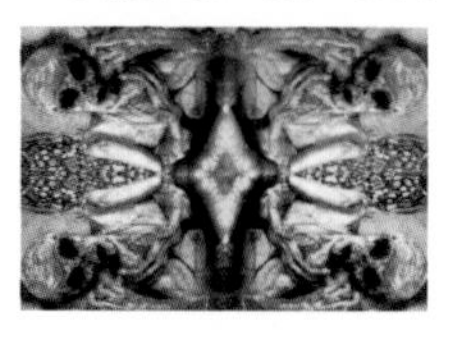

John de Fazio, *Untitled*, 1997; color Xerox; 23¾ x 17¼ inches.

John de Fazio has produced a body of work in different media based on American pop culture images. His film illustrations have appeared in the *New Yorker* magazine, and he has created a number of special projects within the MTV headquarters in Times Square. His work has been exhibited internationally and was included in the 1993 Venice Biennale.

PAGES 40–41:

episode: Anasazi
first aired: May 19, 1995
written by: Chris Carter; story by David Duchovny and Chris Carter
editor: Stephen Mark
directed by: R. W. Goodwin

PAGE 42:

episode: El Mundo Gira
first aired: January 12, 1997
written by: John Shiban
editor: Heather MacDougall
directed by: Tucker Gates

PAGE 43:

Mark Dion, *Untitled*, 1997; Cibachrome print; image size 9½ x 7½ inches; paper size 9 5/16 x 7 15/16 inches.

Born in 1961, Mark Dion is a New York artist whose work in sculpture, installation, performance, and film is about nature and the history of natural science. In particular, he concentrates on the conflicting interactions between humans and the natural world. He is known for his site-specific investigations into biological diversity, including *A Yard of Jungle* at the Museo de Arte Moderna in Rio de Janeiro and *The Great Munich Bug Hunt* at K-Ram Dexter in Munich. Dion has received support from the National Endowment for the Arts and the Lila Wallace and Rockefeller Foundations.

PAGE 44:

Tennessee Rice Dixon, *Letter #3*, 1997; collage; 17⅛ x 11 inches.

Tennessee Rice Dixon works with narrative structures and imagery in book arts, painting, writing, and interactive multimedia. Dixon is co-creator of "ScruTiny in the Great Round," a CD-ROM awarded the Grande Prix du Jury Milia d'Or 96. This work, based on her artist's book of the same title, is a collage of animated images, poetry, and sounds, and tells the story of biotic and spiritual birth. Dixon has illustrated five children's books. She is a professor at City College in the M.F.A. Communications Film Video Department, and teaches in the M.F.A. Computer Art Department at The School of Visual Arts, both in New York City. She is a founding member of Thunder Gulch, a consortium of new media artists and organizations located in New York City.

PAGE 45:

episode: War of the Coprophages
first aired: January 5, 1996
written by: Darin Morgan
editor: Jim Gross
directed by: Kim Manners

PAGES 46–47:

Toni Dove, *Untitled*, 1997; digital color prints (taken from *Artificial Changelings*, an interactive video installation); 30 x 50 inches.

Toni Dove is a performance/installation artist who works with electronic media. She has exhibited installations, artists' books, radio pieces, and performances. She is currently working on *Artificial Changelings*, an interactive narrative laser disk installation that uses video motion sensing to engage viewers in a responsive environment. The piece has been under development since late 1993 and is supported by grants from the National Endowment for the Arts, the New York State Council on the Arts, the New York Foundation for the Arts, Harvestworks, Inc., Art Matters Inc., and the Eugene McDermott Award from MIT.

PAGE 50:

episode: E.B.E.
first aired: February 18, 1994
written by: Glen Morgan and James Wong
editor: Stephen Mark
directed by: William Graham

PAGES 50–51:

Jay Dunn, *Deception Bay Worldwide: two stills from "The Messenger," Lynn Jacobsen, in a film written and directed by Jay Dunn*, 1997; gelatin silver prints; image size 2 11/16 x 8 inches; paper size 8 x 10 inches.

Jay Dunn, a Los Angeles-based filmmaker, musician, and performing artist specializing in video installations, has created over thirty installations for museums and art organizations across the United States. He recently finished directing the surrealist film *Kansas and My Father* and is currently signed to direct two films based on the writings of Antoine de Saint-Exupery.

PAGE 52:

episode: Memento Mori
first aired: February 9, 1997
written by: Chris Carter, Vince Gilligan, John Shiban, and Frank Spotnitz
editor: Michael S. Stern
directed by: Rob Bowman

PAGE 53:

Nicole Eisenman, *Untitled*, 1997; ink and watercolor on paper; 14 1/8 x 10 1/4 inches.

Nicole Eisenman, born in Verdun, France, received her M.F.A. in painting from the Rhode Island School of Design. Her work has been shown in group exhibitions, including *Sexual Politics: Judy Chicago's Dinner Party in Feminist Art History; Defining the Nineties: Consensus-Making in New York, Miami, and Los Angeles; Way Cool;* and *Piccasoid*. She has received a John Simon Guggenheim Fellowship and a Joan Mitchell Foundation grant for her work.

PAGE 54:

Jeanne C. Finley, *Time Bomb*, 1997; digitally manipulated video image; 17 x 22 inches.

Jeanne C. Finley is an artist who works with photography, video, and media installations to explore the intersection between experimental and documentary forms. Finley's videotapes have been broadcast internationally and she has exhibited in museums and festivals throughout the world, including the 1993 and 1995 Whitney Biennials, the Museum of Modern Art in New York, the George Pompidou Center in Paris, the Berlin Film Festival, and the San Francisco Film Festival. She has been the recipient of several grants, including a John Simon Guggenheim Fellowship, a Fulbright Fellowship, and grants from the National Endowment for the Arts. Finley lives in Brooklyn with her husband and daughter.

PAGE 55:

episode: E.B.E.
first aired: February 18, 1994
written by: Glen Morgan and James Wong
editor: Stephen Mark
directed by: William Graham

PAGE 56:

episode: Born Again
first aired: April 29, 1994
written by: Alex Gansa and Howard Gordon
editor: James Coblentz
directed by: Jerrold Freeman

PAGE 57:

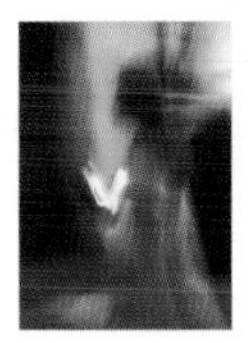

Suzanne Fiol, *The Child Spirit—You Are Empty in Your Body*, 1997; Cibachrome print; image size 22½ x 15¼ inches, paper size 20 x 24 inches.

Suzanne Fiol, a New York artist, studied at the Art Institute of Chicago before receiving her M.F.A. from the Pratt Institute. She has exhibited nationally and her work is included in the permanent collections of the Brooklyn Museum and the Milwaukee Art Museum.

PAGE 58:

episode: El Mundo Gira
first aired: January 12, 1997
written by: John Shiban
editor: Heather MacDougall
directed by: Tucker Gates

PAGE 59:

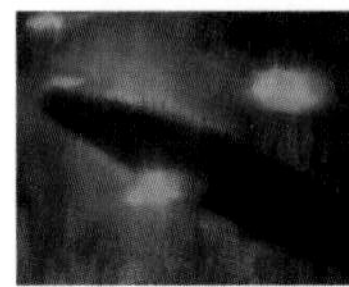

Joy Garnett, *Untitled*, 1997; oil on canvas; 12 x 16 inches.

Joy Garnett received training in environmental biology at McGill University and studied painting at the École des Beaux Arts in Paris. She received her M.F.A. from the City College of New York. Her paintings derive from found science and pseudoscience photography. She lives and works in New York.

PAGE 62:

Michelle Handelman and Monte Cazazza, *Untitled*, from the series *Blood, Guts and Beauty*, 1997; Fujichrome print; image size 9½ x 7$^{5}/_{16}$ inches, frame size 14 x 11 inches.

Michelle Handelman is a filmmaker, writer, and virtual artist. Dealing with the abject body, her work ranges from the irreverent tale of 1970s promiscuity, "Sugar Baby," to her sensitive feature documentary on the lesbian S/M scene. Her films have garnered international critical acclaim and her writing has been published in *Herotica 3*, *Coming Up*, and *Apocalypse Culture*.

Monte Cazazza has been working for fifteen years as an originator and provocateur in the Industrial Culture movement. Appearing in the late 1970s with guerrilla actions involving dead animals, explosives, and painful noise thresholds, Monte has performed with Throbbing Gristle, Psychic TV, and Survival Research Laboratories. Handelman and Cazazza have been collaborating for eight years on film/video/photo projects. Their work is represented by the Catherine Clark Gallery in San Francisco.

PAGE 63:

episode: Sanguinarium
first aired: November 11, 1996
written by: Valerie Mayhew and Vivian Mayhew
editor: Michael S. Stern
directed by: Kim Manners

PAGE 64:

episode: Gethsemane
first aired: May 18, 1997
written by: Chris Carter
editor: Michael S. Stern
directed by: R. W. Goodwin

PAGE 65:

Lyle Ashton Harris, *Untitled (use me)*, 1997; Duraflex print; variable dimensions.

Lyle Ashton Harris, a photographer, has exhibited internationally at the Guggenheim Museum and the Whitney Museum of American Art in New York, Kunsthalle Basel in Switzerland, the Institute of Contemporary Art in London, and the Wexner Center for Arts in Columbus, Ohio. His work can be found in the permanent collections of the Whitney, the Boston Museum of Fine Arts, and the San Diego Museum of Contemporary Art. Harris is represented by Jack Tilton Gallery in New York, and has completed several photography projects for *The New York Times Sunday Magazine*.

PAGE 66:

Julia Heyward, *X666*, 1997; digital color print; image size 7 x 9⅝ inches, paper size 8½ x 11 inches.

Julia Heyward moved to New York in 1973 and began working on video and multimedia performance art while in the Whitney Museum of American Art Independent Study Program. Her work centers around the orchestration of music, image, and language through video and live performance. She has toured with music groups and directed music videos for Sony/CBS, Warner, MCA, Capitol, IRS, and Elektra.

PAGE 67:

episode: Small Potatoes
first aired: April 20, 1997
written by: Vince Gilligan
editor: Heather MacDougall
directed by: Cliff Bole

PAGES 68–69:

episode: Musings of a Cigarette-Smoking Man
first aired: November 17, 1996
written by: Glen Morgan
editor: Jim Gross
directed by: James Wong

PAGE 69:

Brian Horton, *Tiny Secrets*, 1997; digital color print; image size 9 11/16 x 5 7/8 inches, paper size 11 x 8½ inches.

Brian Horton, a professional illustrator and comic book artist working out of North Hollywood, California, has collaborated with Dark Horse Comics on their books *Zombie World* and *Aliens* and has completed a series of paintings for a game inspired by Clive Barker's *Imajica*. A three-year veteran of the video games industry, he is currently working as a background artist on an upcoming Sony Playstation title for Dream Works Interactive.

PAGE 70:

Lisa A. Johnston, *Treatise of Abduction*, 1997; digital multilayered photographic montage; Iris print; 23 x 17 inches.

Lisa A. Johnston, formerly a photojournalist, first became interested in digital photography when she used a computer in her newspaper work. Her digital images have since been exhibited in galleries throughout the United States and in England. Her work can be seen online at the site "Digital Wave Imaging Gallery," which she has been administering since 1994.

PAGE 71:

episode: Duane Barry
first aired: October 14, 1994
written by: Chris Carter
editor: James Coblentz
directed by: Chris Carter

PAGE 74:

episode: Teliko
first aired: October 18, 1996
written by: Howard Gordon
editor: Jim Gross
directed by: James Charleston

PAGE 75:

Joan Jonas, *Untitled*, 1997; color slide; Iris print; 24 x 36 inches.

Joan Jonas, a video performance pioneer, was born in New York City in 1936. She received her B.F.A. in Art History from Mount Holyoke College and earned her M.F.A. from Columbia University. Her work combines elements from the Japanese theater of Kabuki and Noh traditions, modern Western theater, dance, video, and the visual arts. She has produced the video *Organic Honey's Visual Telepathy*, a "television version" of her performance piece *Double Lunar Dogs*, and *Volcano Saga*, a collaborative video-performance with composer Alvin Lucier. She has also performed with The Wooster Group production of *Brace Up* and had a retrospective exhibition at the Stedelijk Museum in Amsterdam. Jonas has been awarded fellowships and grants from the National Endowment for the Arts, the Rockefeller Foundation, the CAT Fund, and the Artist TV Lab at WNET/13 in New York.

PAGE 76:

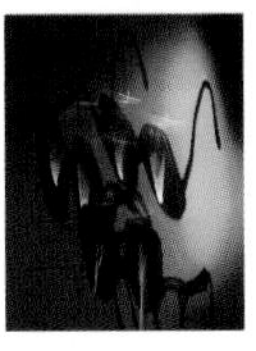

Bill Jones, *Second Sight*, 1997; Cibachrome print (photogram with sunlight and found eyeglasses); 16 x 20 inches.

Bill Jones is an artist who investigates the psychointeractive properties of photography, specifically the possibility of willing images into existence without the aid of a traditional camera. He has had two retrospective shows, *Bill Jones: A Survey* at the Vancouver Art Gallery; and *Bill Jones: Ten Years of Multiple Image Narratives* at the International Center of Photography in New York. Jones lives and works in New York.

PAGES 76–77:

episode: Jose Chung's *From Outer Space*
first aired: April 12, 1996
written by: Darin Morgan
editor: Heather MacDougall
directed by: Rob Bowman

PAGE 78:

episode: Little Green Men
first aired: September 16, 1994
written by: Glen Morgan and James Wong
editor: Stephen Mark
directed by: David Nutter

PAGE 79:

Anne Marie Karlsen, *Guardian*, 1997; photomontage on paper; 16 x 12 inches.

Anne Marie Karlsen, a fine artist, has been involved with the printmaking and painting departments at UCLA for more than a decade. Karlsen's photo montages are highly ordered yet complex images that address our multifaceted perceptions of self and culture. She has exhibited around the country and recently received an artist's grant from the Borchard Foundation for a residency in France. Her work is found in the public collections of the Brooklyn Museum, the Fogg Art Museum, the Museum of Fine Arts in Boston, the Milwaukee Art Museum, the Carnegie Museum of Art, and the Lannan Foundation in Los Angeles, to name a few.

PAGE 80:

Lisa Kereszi, *Eye*, 1997; color slide; Cibachrome print; 16 x 20 inches.

Lisa Kereszi graduated from Bard College in 1995 with a B.F.A. in photography, where she studied with Stephen Shore and Larry Fink. She has worked as an assistant to Nan Goldin, as a freelance photographer, and has been included in several group shows and publications, including a 1996 issue of *Zoom*. She is a part of the traveling Pierogi 2000 flat files, based in the Williamsburg section of Brooklyn, where she lives.

PAGE 81:

episode: Small Potatoes
first aired: April 20, 1997
written by: Vince Gilligan
editor: Heather MacDougall
directed by: Cliff Bole

PAGE 82:

episode: Elegy
first aired: May 4, 1997
written by: John Shiban
editor: Jim Gross
directed by: James Charleston

PAGE 83:

Sean Kilcoyne, *Eidolon*, 1997; digital print; 10 13/16 x 15 7/8 inches.

Sean Kilcoyne, born in 1946, is a performance artist whose works include *Corridors*, *Angels/Anvils*, and *The Boon*. He is currently directing *The Sacred and the Toxic*, an environmentally based work in progress. Kilcoyne's pictures and three-dimensional objects are in numerous private collections.

PAGE 86:

Komar & Melamid, *Watching X-Files*; color Xerox, 35 mm slide for projection; image size 6½ x 10 inches, paper size 8½ x 11 inches.

One of the contemporary art world's most loved duos, Komar & Melamid have been collaborators ever since they met at a Moscow morgue in 1968, when they both studied anatomy at art school. By the early 1970s they had achieved the wildly eclectic inventiveness that is the hallmark of their art. In New York, they swiftly became known for their keen sense of irony and funny satires of Soviet Realism. Komar & Melamid's images are reproduced in countless catalogues and their interviews are often adopted as part of academic curricula. Most recently they have completed their book, *Painting By Numbers*, published by Farrar, Straus and Giroux. Komar & Melamid's work is in the Metropolitan Museum of Art, the Museum of Modern Art, the Stedelijk Museum, the Ludwig Museum, the Guggenheim Museum, and the Whitney Museum of American Art, as well as other public and private collections across the country and around the world.

PAGE 87:

episode: Ghost in the Machine
first aired: October 29, 1993
written by: Alex Gansa and Howard Gordon
editor: James Coblentz
directed by: Jerrold Freeman

PAGE 88:

Barbara Kruger, *Tell Us Something We Don't Know*, 1984; gelatin silver print; 6⅝ x 8 13/16 inches.

Barbara Kruger is an artist whose pictures and words are about issues of power, sex, money, difference, and death. Her work has appeared throughout the United States, Europe, and Japan in galleries, newspapers, magazines, and museums and on billboards, matchbooks, television programs, t-shirts, and shopping bags. She has written about television, film, and culture for *ArtForum*, *Esquire*, the *New York Times*, and the *Village Voice*.

PAGE 89:

episode: Teliko
first aired: October 18, 1996
written by: Howard Gordon
editor: Jim Gross
directed by: James Charleston

PAGE 90:

episode: Humbug
first aired: March 31, 1995
written by: Darin Morgan
editor: James Coblentz
directed by: Kim Manners

PAGE 91:

Paul Lamarre and Melissa Wolf, *Untitled*, 1997; Cibachrome print; 8 x 10 inches.

Paul Lamarre and Melissa Wolf have been working as a collaborative team since 1983, producing art in various media, including objets d'art, video, and installation. Their work is based on the Eidia philosophy, reinterpreting the conventions of empirical experience through selection and objectification of individuality, as seen through randomly occurring acts of expression.

PAGE 92:

Paul Lee, *Untitled*, 1997; acrylic on paper; 15 x 10 inches.

Paul Lee is a painter and a freelance illustrator. On occasion he dabbles in comics. Lee never vacations and is constantly working. Of course for Lee, working consists of lying on the floor in front of the TV and drawing, and generally making a mess at home all day. Lee's other ambition is to become a Duncan Yo-Yo champion and tour the country doing yo-yo tricks. Never satisfied, Lee suffers from the "grass is always greener" syndrome in which he would always rather be doing something else. Lee has recently discovered he doesn't care for winter and hopes to have it outlawed. He expects to win the Lotto soon, and put all this nonsense behind him.

PAGE 93:

episode: Gethsemane
first aired: May 18, 1997
written by: Chris Carter
editor: Michael S. Stern
directed by: R. W. Goodwin

PAGES 94–95:

episode: Sanguinarium
first aired: November 11, 1996
written by: Valerie Mayhew and Vivian Mayhew
editor: Michael S. Stern
directed by: Kim Manners

PAGE 95:

Minnette Lehmann, *Mask Death*, 1997; digital color print; image size 7¾ x 6⅛ inches, paper size 8½ x 11 inches.

Born in Sacramento, California, Minnette Lehmann received her M.F.A. in photography from the San Francisco Art Institute. Her works explore the territories of love, loss, cruelty, and comedy through photographs, performance, and digital media. Her shows include *Nailed* at The Lab in San Francisco, *Christ Mocked Again* at Saint Mary's College, and *Information-Culture-Technology: Roland Barthes'* Camera Lucida at San Francisco State University. Lehmann's works have been exhibited in Prague, Edinburgh, London, Munich, and Amsterdam, and she received a grant for Artist Fellowship in Photography from the National Endowment for the Arts in 1973. She has published writings in *Blind Date*, *Camerawork*, *Photometro*, and *Ink Magazine*, and currently lives in San Francisco.

PAGE 98:

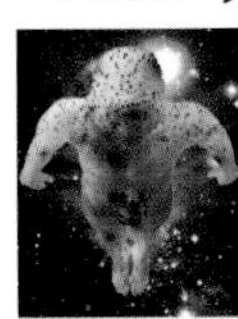

Rudy Lemcke, *Terminus: The Convergence of Matter & Anti-Matter*, 1997; digital print; image size 7¹³⁄₁₆ x 6 inches, paper size 11 x 8½ inches.

Rudy Lemcke, born in St. Louis, Missouri, was educated in philosophy at the University of Louvain in Belgium. He has exhibited in the 10th Annual Dallas Video Festival, *In a Different Light* at the University Art Museum in Berkeley, and at Modernism Gallery in San Francisco.

PAGE 99:

episode: The Field Where I Died
first aired: November 3, 1996
written by: Glen Morgan and James Wong
editor: Heather MacDougall
directed by: Rob Bowman

PAGE 100:

episode: Unruhe
first aired: October 27, 1996
written by: Vince Gilligan
editor: Heather MacDougall
directed by: Rob Bowman

PAGE 101:

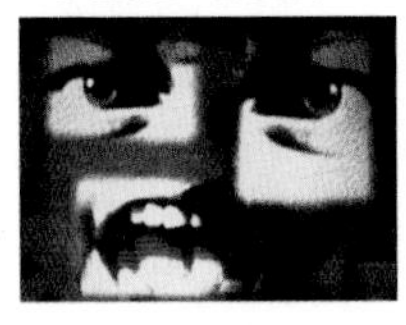

Robert Longo, *Mnemonic Pictures*, 1995; lithograph; 8 x 10 inches.

Brooklyn-born artist Robert Longo borrows images and forms from the media and American society. His early, oversized *Men in the Cities* drawings and the massive multimedia installations brought him international attention, and established him as a prominent figure in the art world during the 1980s. His abstract work in the 1990s included the bronze *Black Flags* and the large-scale *Bodyhammer* gun drawings. Longo has also been involved in directing theater, performance art, opera, rock videos, films, and the feature film adaptation of William Gibson's story "Johnny Mnemonic." His work has been shown in retrospectives at the Los Angeles County Museum of Art, and at the Deichtorhallen in Hamburg. His work is in the collections of the Museum of Modern Art, the Whitney Museum of American Art, and the Guggenheim Museum in New York, the Tate Gallery in London, the Ludwig Collection in Cologne, and Stedelijk in Amsterdam.

PAGE 102:

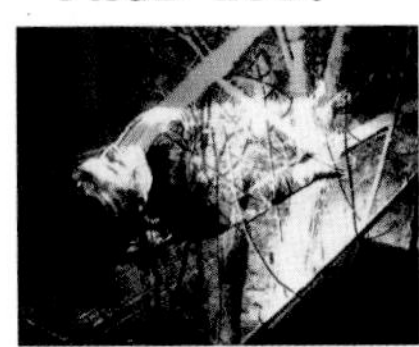

Vera Lutter, *unmarked helicopter*, 1997; gelatin silver print, worked from a projection of pinhole photographs and video stills; image size 7⁵⁄₁₆ x 9⁷⁄₁₆ inches, paper size 7¹⁵⁄₁₆ x 9⅞ inches.

Vera Lutter, born in Germany, studied photography and related media at the School of Visual Arts in New York, where she currently lives. She has shown her installation *Urban Landscapes* at the Marlborough Gallery, *On New York* at Brent Sikkema & Wooster Gardens, and *Insight*, a store window installation, at the Art Association Munich and Galerie X.

PAGE 103:

episode: One Breath
first aired: November 11, 1994
written by: Glen Morgan and James Wong
editor: James Coblentz
directed by: R. W. Goodwin

PAGE 104:

episode: Humbug
first aired: March 31, 1995
written by: Darin Morgan
editor: James Coblentz
directed by: Kim Manners

PAGE 105:

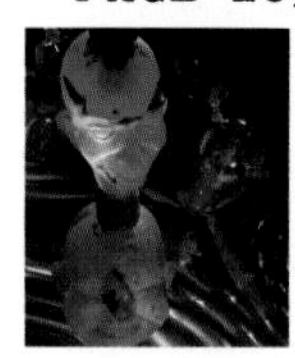

Frank Majore, *Untitled*, 1997; Cibachrome print; 8 x 10 inches.

Frank Majore, born in Richmond Hill, New York, was educated at the Philadelphia College of Art. He has had solo exhibitions in galleries and museums from New York to Los Angeles, and his work is included in the public collections at the International Center of Photography in New York, the Boston Museum of Fine Arts, the Los Angeles County Museum, the Museum of Fine Arts in Houston, and the Whitney Museum of American Art in New York. Majore has received the Aaron Siskind Foundation Photography Fellowship, the Louis Comfort Tiffany Foundation Tiffany Award, and a John Simon Guggenheim Fellowship.

PAGE 106:

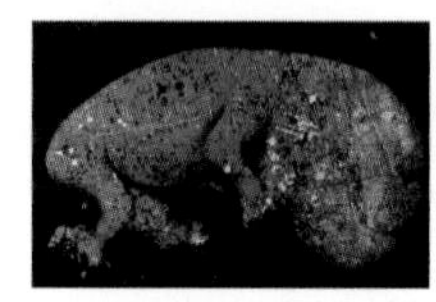

Aline Mare, *Synthesia*, 1997; Ektacolor print; 4 x 5 15/16 inches.

Aline Mare, a mixed-media artist, has produced several works, including *The Book of Flesh*, shown at San Francisco Cinematheque, *S'Aline Solution* at The Kitchen in New York, *Woman and the Body* at the Massachusetts College of Arts and *Body of Desire* at the London Film Co-op. She received the 1996 BAVC Award and is currently working on a new media project called *The Breathing Breast*.

PAGE 107:

episode: The Erlenmeyer Flask
first aired: May 13, 1994
written by: Chris Carter
editor: Heather MacDougall
directed by: R. W. Goodwin

PAGE 110:

episode: Humbug
first aired: March 31, 1995
written by: Darin Morgan
editor: James Coblentz
directed by: Kim Manners

PAGE 111:

Clay Patrick McBride, *Untitled* (inspired by the *X-Files* episode "Home"), 1997; gelatin silver print; 19 3/4 x 15 13/16 inches.

Clay Patrick McBride was born in Goshen, New York, and studied painting and drawing in France before receiving his B.F.A. from the School of Visual Arts in New York. He has been included in several exhibitions in New York and Europe. His work has been collected by other artists, including Joel Peter Witkin and Mark Elliot Lugo. Currently, he is working as a photo illustrator for book publishers, magazines, and record companies.

PAGES 112–113:

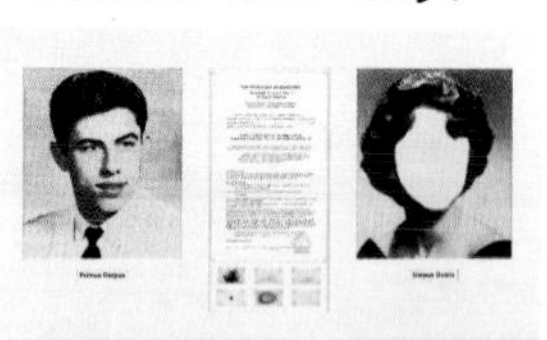

Larry Miller, *Genome License No. 7 (Corpus Dualis)*, 1997; black-and-white photographs, text and rubber stamp, polyethylene bags, hair, fingernails, tooth slice, and blood of the artist, hair and toenails of the artist's mother; 23 1/2 x 43 1/4 inches.

Larry Miller, an artist with a background in theater, music, and the visual arts, began his association with the international Fluxus group in 1969. During the 1970s, he was identified with the emerging wave of artists developing performance and installation art. He was one of the first artists to signal the cultural impact of the oncoming genetics revolution by declaring copyright ownership of his own DNA [*Only One*] in 1989. His work has been exhibited at the Whitney Museum of American Art, the New Museum and the Museum of Modern Art in New York; the Walker Art Center in Minneapolis; the Museum of Contemporary Art in Chicago; the San Francisco Museum of Modern Art; and in the 1990 Venice Biennale.

PAGE 113:

episode: Demons
first aired: May 11, 1997
written by: R. W. Goodwin
editor: Heather MacDougall
directed by: Kim Manners

PAGE 114:

episode: Musings of a Cigarette-Smoking Man
first aired: November 17, 1996
written by: Glen Morgan
editor: Jim Gross
directed by: James Wong

PAGES 114-115:

John Monteith, *Untitled*, 1997; collage; 12⅜ x 16⅞ inches.

John Monteith is a self-taught artist who was raised in the north-east and educated at Texas Tech University, where he studied to be a pathologist. Over the past twelve years, he has been making collages with class pictures mostly from year-books published by the University of South Carolina.

PAGE 116:

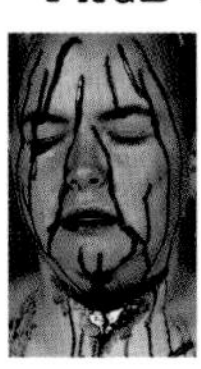

Catherine Opie, *Untitled*, 1997; gelatin silver print; image size 9½ x 5⁹⁄₁₆ inches, paper size 10 x 8 inches.

Catherine Opie studied at the San Francisco Art Institute, where she received her B.F.A., and went on to earn her M.F.A. from CalArts. She is represented by Regen Projects in Los Angeles and has had several solo exhibitions, including *Catherine Opie* at the Museum of Contemporary Art in Los Angeles, and *Houses and Freeways*, shown at both Ginza Art Space in Tokyo and Jay Gorney Modern Art in New York. Among her group exhibitions are *Identity Crisis: Self Portraiture at the End of the Century* at the Milwaukee Art Museum; *Sunshine & Noir: Art in L.A. 1960-1997* at the Louisiana Museum in Humlebaek, Denmark; and *Spheres of Influence* at the Museum of Contemporary Art in Los Angeles. Opie has also shown at the Guggenheim Museum, Whitney Museum of American Art in New York, the Museum of Fine Arts in Boston, the Photographers Gallery in London, and the Center on Contemporary Art in Seattle. Opie currently lives and works in Los Angeles.

PAGE 117:

episode: Elegy
first aired: May 4, 1997
written by: John Shiban
editor: Jim Gross
directed by: James Charleston

PAGE 118:

episode: Never Again
first aired: February 2, 1997
written by: Glen Morgan and James Wong
editor: Jim Gross
directed by: Rob Bowman

PAGE 119:

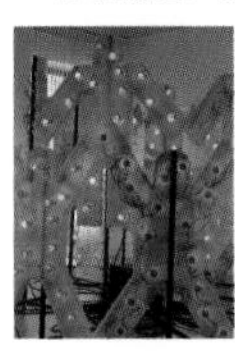

Dennis Oppenheim, *Go Surrounded by Stop*, 1997; cast fiberglass, steel, electrical fixtures, light bulbs, lighting controller, electric wire; 12 feet high x 40 feet long x 40 feet diameter.

Dennis Oppenheim, born in Electric City, Washington, studied at the School of Arts and Crafts at Oakland, California, before receiving his M.F.A. from Stanford University in 1966. He has lived and worked in New York since 1967 and has had solo exhibitions at the Tate Gallery in London, the Stedelijk Museum in Amsterdam, the Musee d'Art Moderne de la Ville de Paris, the Rijksmuseum Kroller-Muller in Otterlo, Holland, the San Francisco Museum of Modern Art, and at P.S. 1 Contemporary Art Center in New York.

PAGE 122:

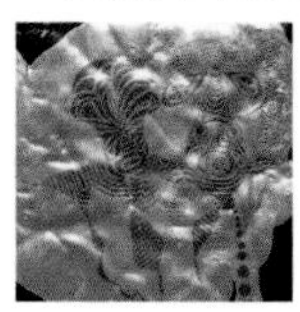

Marc Pally, *Let X Equal X*, 1997; graphite, colored pencil, and acrylic on canvas; 5 x 5 inches.

Marc Pally, born and living in Los Angeles, received his M.F.A. from the California Institute of the Arts in Valencia. He has held solo exhibitions at the Ulrike Kantor Gallery in Los Angeles, the Rosemund Felsen Gallery in San Diego, the Los Angeles Institute of Contemporary Art, US Irvine Fine Arts Gallery, and Newport Harbor Art Museum in Newport Beach. His work has been included in group exhibitions in Los Angeles at the Los Angeles County Museum of Art, the Otis School of Art and Design, and the Museum of Contemporary Art (MOCA), and is in the permanent collections of the Museum of Contemporary Art in Los Angeles and the Newport Harbor Art Museum. Pally has held the position of director for Los Angeles Contemporary Exhibitons (LACE) and teaches at Art Center College of Design in Pasadena.

PAGE 123:

episode: Conduit
first aired: October 1, 1993
written by: Alex Gansa and Howard Gordon
editor: James Coblentz
directed by: Daniel Sackheim

PAGE 124:

episode: Demons
first aired: May 11, 1997
written by: R. W. Goodwin
editor: Heather MacDougall
directed by: Kim Manners

PAGE 125:

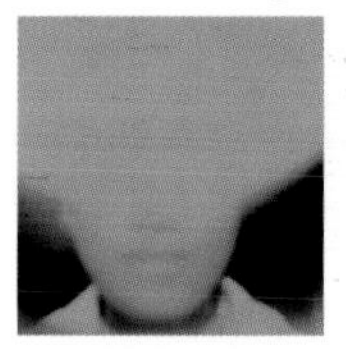

Barbara Pollack, *A Page from Agent Mulder's Family Album*, 1996; polaroid photo printed in Cibachrome; 4½ x 3½ inches.

Barbara Pollack is an artist who lives and works in New York. Her exhibit, *Barbara Pollack*, was held at the Holly Solomon Gallery in New York. She has also shown in group exhibitions, *In the Flow* at Franklin Furnace, *Have a Heart* at Castelli Graphics, and at the New Museum in New York. She has been involved in online projects, including the website "Talkback! Long Distance Art & Culture" and the Moo space "Oracle."

PAGES 126-127:

Daniel Reiser, *Untitled*, 1996; Cibachrome print; image size 18 x 36⅛ inches, mount size 32¾ x 39¹⁵⁄₁₆ inches.

Daniel Reiser is represented by John Gibson Gallery in New York City. He has exhibited in avant-garde alternative spaces, including the Franklin Furnace and Thread Waxing Space in New York as well as Pierogi 2000 in Brooklyn. His work has been shown in France, Spain, and Italy. In 1996 he was invited to exhibit at the Recontres Internationales de la Photographie, and in 1997 his work traveled with a group exhibition, *"Doll Houses" Children in Chrisis*, through Germany. The proceeds from admissions to the show were donated to the children of Bosnia-Herzegovina. His work is in the permanent collection of the Museum of Modern Art in New York.

PAGES 128-129:

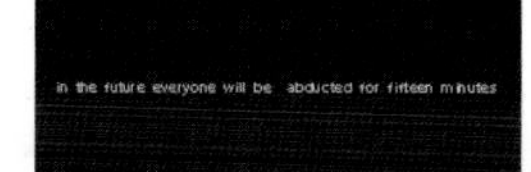

David Robbins, *In the future everyone will be abducted for fifteen minutes*; variable dimensions.

David Robbins is an artist and writer currently living in Chicago. He has had twenty-one person exhibitions in the U.S. and Europe, and is the author of three collections of essays and interviews: *The Camera Believes Everything* (1988), *Foundation Papers from the Archives of the Institute for Advanced Comedic Behavior* (1992), and *The Dr. Frankenstein Option* (1993). A collection of his short fiction will be published in 1998. David Robbins would like to credit David McWeeney, who orginated the remark "In the future everyone will be abducted for fifteen minutes."

PAGE 130:

David C. Scher, *Monotremes Unite!*, 1997; ink and watercolor on paper; 8½ x 9⅝ inches.

David C. Scher, born in St. Louis, Missouri, has exhibited in Cologne, Budapest, Venice, London, Berlin, at Pierogi 2000 in New York, Four Walls and Jack Tilton Gallery. He is cofounder of Lint Bucket. His "Old Moth" is at http://4worlds.com/wib.

PAGE 131:

episode: Apocrypha
first aired: February 16, 1996
written by: Frank Spotnitz and Chris Carter
editor: Stephen Mark
directed by: Kim Manners

PAGE 134:

episode: Redux
first aired: November 2, 1997
written by: Chris Carter
editor: Heather MacDougall
directed by: R. W. Goodwin

PAGE 135:

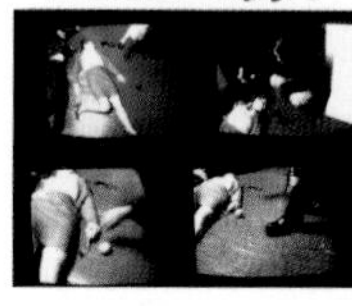

Julia Scher, *Untitled*, 1997; digital color print; 10¾ x 14 inches.

Julia Scher, born in Hollywood, California, has exhibited, performed, written, and recorded her work. She has appeared in numerous exhibitions, including *Predictive Engineering II* at the San Francisco Museum of Art, *Security World* at the Galerie Ghislaine Hussenot in Paris, *Surveillance* at the Massachusetts Institute of Technology, and *Performance Anxiety* and *So You Wanna Be A Rock and Roll Star*, both at the Museum of Contemporary Art in Chicago. She has also produced performances, *In-security by Julia* and *Women in Prison*; online exhibitions, "Information America," "Securityland," and "Wonderland"; has been published in books, *The Power of Feminist Art* and *Techno-Culture*; and directed radio and television broadcasts and audio recordings.

PAGE 136:

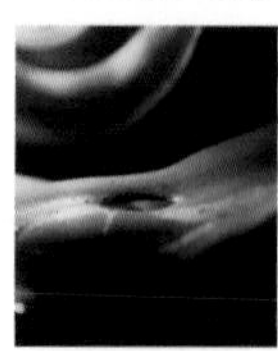

John Schlesinger, *Untitled*, 1997; gelatin silver print; image size 20 x 17½ inches, paper size 24 x 20 inches.

John Schlesinger has shown in solo exhibitions at Julie Saul Gallery, White Columns in New York, Camera Work in San Francisco, Van Rooy Gallery in the Netherlands, and in group exhibitions such as *The Real Big Picture* at the Queens Museum. Educated at the University of Minnesota, he has a B.S. in art education and a B.F.A. in photography and philosophy. His work is included in the collections of the Art Institute of Chicago, the Dallas Museum of Fine Arts, the Museum of Modern Art in New York, the Minneapolis Institute of Art, and the San Francisco Museum of Modern Art. Schlesinger has received two National Endowment for the Arts Fellowships and the Aaron Siskind Foundation Photography Fellowship. John Shlesinger's work appears courtesy of Julie Saul Gallery.

PAGE 137:

episode: 3
first aired: November 4, 1994
written by: Chris Ruppenthal, Glen Morgan, and James Wong
editor: Stephen Mark
directed by: David Nutter

PAGE 138:

episode: Terma
first aired: December 1, 1996
written by: Frank Spotnitz and Chris Carter
editor: Jim Gross
directed by: Rob Bowman

PAGE 139:

Collier Schorr, *Soldiers Bathing, Schwabisch Gmund*, 1996; C-print; 18 x 24 inches.

Collier Schorr was born in New York City and studied at the School of Visual Arts. Her work has been presented in group exhibitions, including *Ideal Standard Life* at the Spiral Wacoal Center in Tokyo; *Persona* at the Renaissance Society in Chicago; *Images of Masculinity* at the Victoria Miro Gallery in London; the Whitney Museum of American Art in New York; the Aldrich Museum of Contemporary Art in Ridgefield, Connecticut; and the Museum of Contemporary Art in Los Angeles. Her writings have been published in *frieze* and *Artforum*.

PAGE 140:

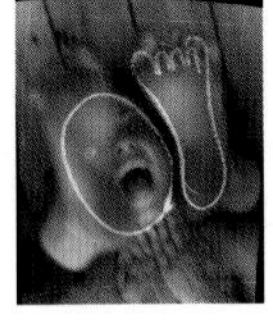

Gerald Slota, *Untitled*, 1997; gelatin silver print; image size 30⅙ x 23¾ inches.

Gerald Slota was born in 1965 and raised in Pompton Lakes, New Jersey, a suburb that has inspired much of his work. He is fascinated with what he calls "the essence of the way everything seems to be or is supposed to be." Slota was drawn to photography by the idea that what is captured on film actually existed, that it is "true."

PAGE 141:

episode: Home
first aired: October 11, 1996
written by: Glen Morgan and James Wong
editor: Michael S. Stern
directed by: Kim Manners

PAGE 142:

episode: Unrequited
first aired: February 23, 1997
written by: Howard Gordon and Chris Carter; story by Howard Gordon
editor: Jim Gross
directed by: Michael Lange

PAGE 143:

Rose Stasuk, *Blindspot*, 1997; digital color print; image size 8 x 10 inches, paper size 8½ x 11 inches.

Rose Stasuk, a digital artist, maintains a World Wide Web project called "The Body Internet" from her studio computer in central Florida. Her work is included in several online databases, including Sonoma State University's "Women Artists Archive," the "Varo Artists Registry," and Arizona State University's "Women On-Line." She was awarded the 1995-96 Individual Artist Fellowship from the state of Florida for interdisciplinary art.

PAGE 146:

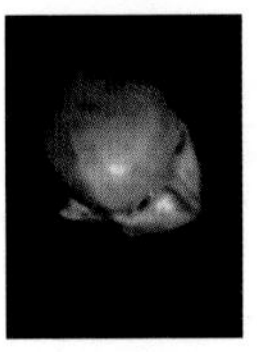

Robert Stivers, *Untitled*, 1995-1997; gelatin silver print; image size 11 x 9 inches, paper size 11 x 14 inches.

Robert Stivers's photographs have been exhibited internationally and are in the collections of the Los Angeles County Museum of Art, the Museum Ludwig in Cologne, and the Victoria and Albert Museum in London. His first monograph, *Robert Stivers, Photographs*, was published in 1997 by Arena Editions.

PAGE 147:

episode: Leonard Betts
first aired: January 26, 1997
written by: Vince Gilligan, John Shiban, and Frank Spotnitz
editor: Heather MacDougall
directed by: Kim Manners

PAGE 148:

Oliver Wasow, *Untitled #313*, 1997; Iris print; image size 5⅞ x 8 inches.

Oliver Wasow, born in Madison, Wisconsin, was educated at Hunter College and the New School for Social Research in New York. He has participated in numerous exhibitions, including *Photography of Invention* at the National Museum of Art in Washington, D.C., and *Astronomy, Optics and Outer Space* at the Ansel Adams Center for Photography in San Francisco. He has also worked on *Los Alamos Wisconsin*, *Kitt Peak*, a limited artists' book; and *Doll House Party*, a collaborative digital project for *The New York Times Magazine*. His work is found in the public collections of the Milwaukee Art Museum, the Museum of Modern Art in New York, and the Whitney Museum of American Art in New York.

PAGE 149:

episode: Home
first aired: October 11, 1996
written by: Glen Morgan and James Wong
editor: Michael S. Stern
directed by: Kim Manners

PAGES 150–151:

Jill Waterman, *Darkness Into Light Turning Red & Green, Rosendale, NY*, 1997; C-print; small format 6 x 9 inches, large format 8 x 10 inches.

Jill Waterman, a photographer living in New York since 1985, was a founder of 494 Gallery, an artist-run gallery in Soho. Her recent work addresses issues of contemporary mythology. Waterman's photographic installations were recognized in 1995 when she was named a finalist for a National Endowment for the Arts Mid-Atlantic Arts Foundation Fellowship.

PAGE 151:

episode: Musings of a Cigarette-Smoking Man
first aired: November 17, 1996
written by: Glen Morgan
editor: Jim Gross
directed by: James Wong

PAGES 152–153:

episode: Grotesque
first aired: February 2, 1996
written by: Howard Gordon
editor: Heather MacDougall
directed by: Kim Manners

PAGE 153:

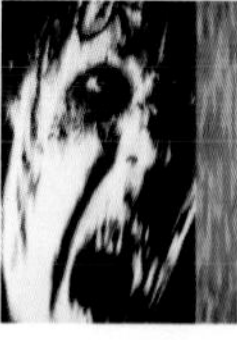

Ken Weaver, *Excoriating Abdominal Emanation: Fear Actualized*, 1997; oil on canvas; 42¼ x 32⅛ inches.

Ken Weaver, born in Palm Beach, studied at the University of Florida before receiving his M.F.A. from Long Island University. He has been featured in exhibitions in Los Angeles at Tom Solomon's Garage, and in New York at Tony Shafrazi Gallery, Barbara Gladstone Gallery, Virtual Space, Franklin Furnace, La Mama, and the Knitting Factory. He has received a grant from the National Endowment for the Humanities.

PAGE 154:

Patty Wickman, *(Within) Without*, 1993; oil on canvas; 60 x 42 inches.

Patty Wickman was born in Pasadena, California, and studied at Arizona State University, Tempe, where she received a B.F.A., and at the University of Colorado, Boulder, where she received an M.F.A. She has held solo exhibitions at Dan Bernier Gallery in Santa Monica and Los Angeles Contemporary Exhibitions in Los Angeles. Group exhibitions include *CA90001-185* at W-139 in Amsterdam, *Be Specific* at Rosamund Felsen Gallery in Santa Monica, and *LAX: The Los Angeles Exhibition* at the Los Angeles Municipal Gallery. Wickman is currently an Associate Professor of Art at the University of California, Los Angeles.

PAGES 154–155:

episode: Teliko
first aired: October 18, 1996
written by: Howard Gordon
editor: Jim Gross
directed by: James Charleston

PAGE 156:

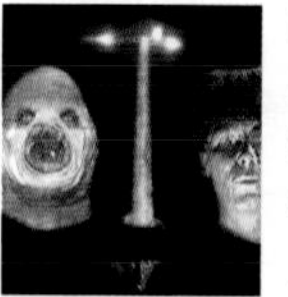

Bruce and Norman Yonemoto, *The Kappa X-File*, 1997; digital color print; image size 10 x 7 15/16 inches, paper size 11 x 8½ inches.

Bruce and Norman Yonemoto, Los Angeles–based media artists, work with film, video, and multimedia installations to explore how living in a continuous, seamless, and ethnocentric mass media environment affects personal and political identity. Their work has been shown internationally and is in the permanent collections of the Museum of Modern Art in New York, Cornell University, and the Hara Museum of Contemporary Art in Tokyo. Recipients of the Maya Deren Award for Independent Film and Video Artists, the Yonemoto brothers have just completed *Japan in Paris in L.A.*, a film about "the Van Gogh of Japan," Saeki Yuzo. They are currently preparing for a midcareer retrospective at the Japanese American National Museum in Los Angeles, scheduled for the spring of 1998.

PAGES 156–157:

episode: El Mundo Gira
first aired: January 12, 1997
written by: John Shiban
editor: Heather MacDougall
directed by: Tucker Gates

PAGE 158:

episode: Never Again
first aired: February 2, 1997
written by: Glen Morgan and James Wong
editor: Jim Gross
directed by: Rob Bowman

Voyager
An imprint of HarperCollins*Publishers*
77-85 Fulham Palace Road,
Hammersmith, London W6 8JB

First published in Great Britain 1998
9 8 7 6 5 4 3 2 1

Photographs on pages 1, 4, 5 and 175 by David Hughes/Hotfoot Studio

Designed by Tanya Ross-Hughes/Hotfoot Studio

The Art of The X-Files is produced by Lookout and The M. Company & Friends

Lookout
1024 Avenue of the Americas
New York, NY 10018
212-221-6463

The M. Company & Friends
2029 Ashland Avenue
Santa Monica, CA 90405
310-450-4691

A catalogue record for this book is available from the British Library

ISBN 0 00 255886 6

Printed and bound in China